CAMPAIGN • 204

THE SECOND CRUSADE 1148

Disaster outside Damascus

DAVID NICOLLE

ILLUSTRATED BY CHRISTA HOOK

Series editors Marcus Cowper and Nikolai Bogdanovic

First published in 2009 by Osprey Publishing
Midland House, West Way, Botley, Oxford OX2 0PH, UK
443 Park Avenue South, New York, NY 10016, USA
E-mail: info@ospreypublishing.com

A CIP catalogue record for this book is available from the British Library.

Print ISBN: 978 1 84603 354 4
PDF e-book ISBN: 978 1 84603 822 8

Editorial by Ilios Publishing Ltd, Oxford, UK (www.iliospublishing.com)
Page layout by: The Black Spot
Typeset in Sabon and Myriad Pro
Index by Fineline Editorial Services
Originated by United Graphic Pte Ltd., Singapore
Cartography: The Map Studio
Bird's-eye view artworks: The Black Spot
Printed in China through Worldprint Ltd.

09 10 11 12 13   9 8 7 6 5 4 3 2 1

FOR A CATALOGUE OF ALL BOOKS PUBLISHED BY OSPREY MILITARY AND
AVIATION PLEASE CONTACT:

NORTH AMERICA
Osprey Direct, c/o Random House Distribution Center, 400 Hahn Road,
Westminster, MD 21157
E-mail: uscustomerservice@ospreypublishing.com

ALL OTHER REGIONS
Osprey Direct, The Book Service Ltd, Distribution Centre, Colchester Road,
Frating Green, Colchester, Essex, CO7 7DW, UK

E-mail: customerservice@ospreypublishing.com

www.ospreypublishing.com

DEDICATION

For Sophie Berthier, Archéologue and Malikah al-Qal'ah.

ARTIST'S NOTE

Readers may care to note that the original paintings from which the
colour plates in this book were prepared are available for private sale.
The Publishers retain all reproduction copyright whatsoever. All enquiries
should be addressed to:

Scorpio Gallery, PO Box 475, Hailsham, East Sussex BN27 2SL, UK

The Publishers regret that they can enter into no correspondence upon
this matter.

THE WOODLAND TRUST

Osprey Publishing are supporting the Woodland Trust, the UK's leading
woodland conservation charity, by funding the dedication of trees.

Key to military symbols

×××××	××××	×××	××	×	III	II
Army Group	Army	Corps	Division	Brigade	Regiment	Battalion

I		•		**Key to unit identification**
Company/Battery	Infantry	Artillery	Cavalry	

Unit
identifier   Parent
unit
Commander
(+) with added elements
(−) less elements

CONTENTS

The many fronts of the Second Crusade 1147–49 (frontiers c. 1147)

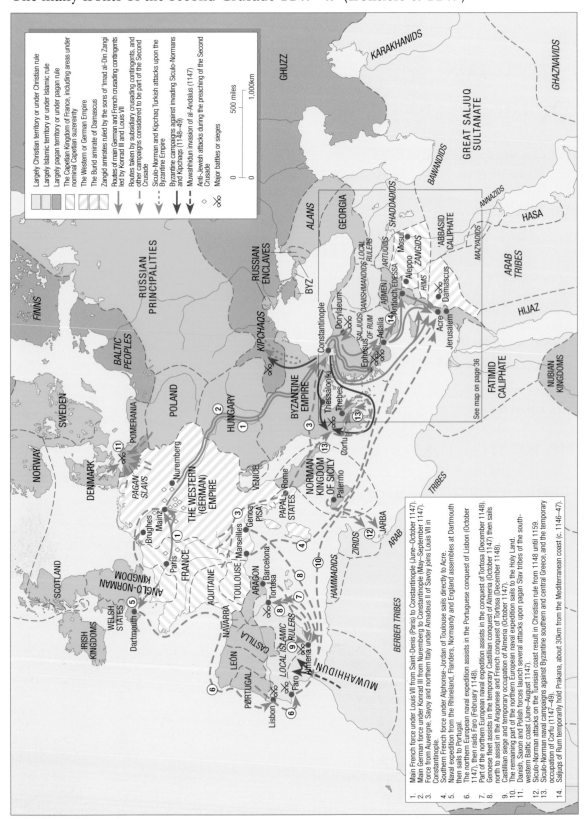

Legend:

- Largely Christian territory or under Christian rule
- Largely Islamic territory or under Islamic rule
- Largely pagan territory or under pagan rule
- The Capetian Kingdom of France, including areas under nominal Capetian suzereinty
- The Western or German Empire
- The Burid amirate of Damascus
- Zangid amirates ruled by the sons of 'Imad al-Din Zangi
- Routes of main German and French crusading contingents led by Konrad III and Louis VII
- Routes taken by subsidiary crusading contingents, and other campaigns considered to be part of the Second Crusade
- Siculo-Norman and Kipchaq Turkish attacks upon the Byzantine Empire
- Byzantine campaigns against invading Siculo-Normans and Kipchaqs (1148–49)
- Muwahhidun invasion of al-Andalus (1147)
- Anti-Jewish attacks during the preaching of the Second Crusade
- Major battles or sieges

0 500 miles

0 500 1,000km

See map on page 36

1. Main French force under Louis VII from Saint-Denis (Paris) to Constantinople (June–October 1147).
2. Main German force under Konrad III from Nuremberg to Constantinople (May–September 1147).
3. Force from Auvergne, Savoy and northern Italy under Amadeus II of Savoy joins Louis VII in Constantinople.
4. Southern French force under Alphonse-Jordan of Toulouse sails directly to Acre.
5. Naval expedition from the Rhineland, Flanders, Normandy and England assembles at Dartmouth then sails to Portugal.
6. The northern European naval expedition assists in the Portuguese conquest of Lisbon (October 1147), then raids Faro (February 1148).
7. Part of the northern European naval expedition assists in the temporary Castilian conquest of Tortosa (December 1148); then sails north to assist in the Aragonese and French conquest of Tortosa (December 1148).
8. Genoese fleet assists in the temporary Castilian conquest of Almeria (October 1147) then sails north to assist in the Aragonese and French conquest of Tortosa (December 1148).
9. Castilian siege and temporary occupation of Almeria (October 1147).
10. The remaining part of the northern European naval expedition sails to the Holy Land.
11. Danish, Saxon and Polish forces launch several attacks upon pagan Slav tribes of the south-western Baltic coast (June–August 1147).
12. Siculo-Norman attacks on the Tunisian coast result in Christian rule from 1148 until 1159.
13. Siculo-Norman naval campaigns against Byzantine southern and central Greece; and the temporary occupation of Corfu (1147–49).
14. Saljuqs of Rum temporarily hold Prakana, about 30km from the Mediterranean coast (c. 1146–47).

INTRODUCTION

The immediate reason for the launching of the Second Crusade was the Islamic reconquest of the city of Edessa (Urfa), marking the collapse of the first Crusader State to be established and the first to fall. However, the Crusader States established in the Middle East as a result of the First Crusade in 1099 had already seen setbacks. The first major defeat suffered by the crusader settlers or, as they were known in the Middle East, the 'Franks' had been as early as 1119 at the catastrophic battle of the Field of Blood. There were, of course, also significant victories, and only five years after the Field of Blood the Kingdom of Jerusalem seized the port city of Tyre. Though Tyre had been nominally under the rule of the Fatimid Caliphate of Egypt, its fall was equally important for the Islamic city of Damascus, which could thereafter trade with the Mediterranean only through crusader-held ports.

Around 1125 a young German nobleman named Konrad is understood to have served as a 'guest knight' in the Kingdom of Jerusalem. It is unclear how long he stayed, but he may well have taken part in King Baldwin II of Jerusalem's raid deep into the territory of Damascus during the autumn of

It took many years for the idea of 'counter-crusading' to take root, and Islamic civilization retained its peaceful character, especially amongst the Arab elites, as illustrated in this 11th- or 12th-century wooden door panel from the Fatimid palace in Cairo. (Museum of Islamic Art, Cairo; author's photograph)

that year. He may even have taken part in the attempt to seize Damascus itself the following January. Just over 20 years later Konrad would return, this time as King of Germany, acknowledged (though uncrowned) as emperor, and the most senior commander in the Second Crusade.

There were few clearly defined frontiers separating the Crusader States and their Islamic neighbours, and this was particularly true of the area between the crusader Kingdom of Jerusalem and the independent *amirate* or principality of Damascus. In fact, the area around the upper Jordan River, eastern Galilee, the Golan Heights and the Hawran region around the Yarmuk River was more like a zone of separation in which each side held a number of strongpoints from which they attempted to impose their authority on neighbouring villages and Arab tribes.

In addition to strategic and military considerations, the Crusader States faced internal and external political strains. The County of Edessa was the most exposed and vulnerable of these Western European colonial creations. It was also the most dependent upon local Christian, particularly Armenian, support. Meanwhile, the Principality of Antioch never quite escaped the threat of Byzantine domination. In several ways the Principality of Antioch was already becoming separate from its Frankish neighbours to the south, at least in terms of its political and military priorities. These factors would have a profound impact upon the course of the Second Crusade.

The abbey church of La Madeleine at Vézelay in central France where King Louis VII of France took the cross before departing on crusade. (Author's photograph)

Meanwhile political tensions within the Kingdom of Jerusalem laid the foundations for the failure of the Second Crusade and for the eventual fall of the kingdom. The same year that the Franks launched another unsuccessful assault against Damascus (1129), a French nobleman named Fulk of Anjou arrived and married Melisende, the eldest daughter of King Baldwin II of Jerusalem and his designated heir. Two years later Baldwin II died, and Melisende became queen with Fulk as king. Unfortunately, Fulk of Anjou refused to share power with his queen, rewarded his French followers with senior positions and drew the kingdom into an increasing powerful Angevin (meaning 'of Anjou') network that would eventually include England under its first Angevin king, Henry II. Meanwhile many of the local barons of the crusader kingdom rallied in support of Queen Melisende, feeling their own positions to be under threat.

Meanwhile this period also saw the beginning of the power of the Military Orders, the Hospitallers gaining the castle of Bethgibelin (Bayt Jibrin) while the Templars were granted frontier territory in the Amanus Mountains. Relations with the neighbouring Islamic states were not always unfriendly, aided by a mutual interest in trade.

Compared with events in the other Crusader States, the County of Tripoli seemed relatively stable, though in 1137 Count Pons was killed during an invasion by Damascus. He was succeeded by Raymond II of Tripoli, who was unable to stop 'Imad al-Din Zangi, the

increasingly powerful ruler of northern Iraq and northern Syria, from conquering the castle of Montferrand and capturing Count Raymond II himself. 'Imad al-Din Zangi campaigned against both the Islamic and Crusader States, and just before taking Montferrand he had unsuccessfully besieged Hims, which formed part of the rival Islamic state of Damascus. Meanwhile, Damascus retained a precarious independence from both the Kingdom of Jerusalem and 'Imad al-Din Zangi. Competion for domination of Damascus would be the primary factor in the Second Crusade.

Events came to a head in the mid-1140s. On 7 November 1143 King Fulk of Jerusalem was killed in Acre; on Christmas Day his adolescent son was crowned as Baldwin III. For the next few years power was largely in the hands of his formidable mother, Queen Melisende, but as soon as Baldwin III came of age relations with his mother deteriorated. Having already been joint ruler with King Fulk of Anjou, Queen Melisende was clearly unwilling to release the reins of power. The resulting tensions divided the kingdom between supporters of Baldwin III and Melisende, and would eventually lead to civil war in 1152.

Important as the Crusades and Crusader States were in the eyes of Western Europeans, they were still of minor importance to the wider Islamic world. In fact, the increasing attempts by local Muslim rulers to roll back the 'Frankish' conquests often had more to do with Islamic political and religious rivalries than with the actual threat posed by Western invaders. The political and religious situation with the Islamic Middle East and farther east was extraordinarily fluid, with events being linked across a huge area. The result was a daunting degree of infighting during the first half of the 12th century. Above all there was the rivalry between the Sunni and Shi'a branches of Islam, which, though far from new, was particularly bitter during the first half of the 12th century. It lay behind the establishment of the first Sunni *madrasas* or religious colleges in Syria – the first in Damascus dating from 1103 and the first in Aleppo from 1123. They were not primarily concerned

Twelfth-century Damascus was much smaller than today's city. The old medieval city, with the Great Umayyad Mosque at its centre, is seen here from Muhajirun, on the slopes of Mount Qasyun. (Author's photograph)

The military equipment used by the warriors of the Second Crusade was much the same as that used on the First Crusade, as seen in this mid-20th-century copy of a now lost mid-12th-century French wall painting from the church of Notre Dame du Mont Carmel in Areines. (Musée des Monuments Français, Paris)

with the Christian crusader threat but were intended to strengthen Sunni vis-à-vis Shi'a Islam. Only later did they become a focus for the preaching of an anti-crusader jihad, previous calls to Sunni jihad having largely been aimed at the Shi'a.

In the very early 12th century, when Arab Syria seemed to be threatened by Muslim Turks and Christian 'Franks', many Sunni as well as Shi'a Muslims saw the Isma'ilis as the only force capable of challenging these foreigners. The Isma'ilis were themselves a branch of the already fragmented Shi'a, though they had the advantage of being represented by a major, if militarily declining, state – the Fatimid Caliphate in Egypt. Despite fragmentation and bitter rivalry within the Isma'ili branch of Shi'a Islam, the Isma'ilis were for a while powerful, operating mainly from Aleppo and then from Damascus between 1113 and 1130. Between 1130 and 1151 the Nizari or Nusayri branch of the Isma'ilis won control of a number of mountain fortresses in the Jabal Ansariyya on the frontier with the Crusader States of northern Syria. This period spanned that of the Second Crusade, but, even before the crusader assault on Damascus in 1148, the Nusayri-Isma'ilis had been closely involved in the complex relationship between Damascus and Jerusalem.

Late in 1129 anti-Isma'ili feelings resulted in a massacre of Nusayris in Damascus, which was probably instigated by the ruler of the principality, Taj al-Muluk Buri – he himself being assassinated in 1131. Meanwhile, many Isma'ilis fled to the northern mountains where, in 1140 or 1141, they captured the fortress town of Masyaf. This henceforth became the effective capital of an Isma'ili mini-state in the mountains – better-known amongst Western historians as the 'Assassin' state.

The story of Damascus and its dependent territories from the time of the First Crusade to that of the Second was largely one of emerging independence followed by the struggle to retain it. In 1123 the death of Sultan Shah Ibn Ridwan, the Saljuq Turkish ruler of Syria, resulted in the *atabeg* (or 'prince's father-figure') Tughtigin becoming ruler rather than merely governor of Damascus. He was succeeded by his son Buri, after whom the independent Burid dynasty of Damascus is named. In 1132, Isma'il Ibn Buri became ruler of Damascus, being replaced by his brother Mahmud Ibn Buri in 1135. From then on, however, the authority of the ruling prince declined while that of a new *atabeg* and army commander increased.

Meanwhile the rising power of 'Imad al-Din Zangi of Mosul in the north was causing even greater concern to Damascus than it was to the Crusader States. 'Imad al-Din Zangi was a clever politician as well as a successful military leader. His marriage to Mahmud Ibn Buri's widowed mother, the formidable Zumurrud Khatun, resulted in the frontier city of Hims being handed over peacefully to Zangi. This arrangement also seems to have been an acknowledgement of Zangi's military superiority. In June 1139 Mahmud was murdered and so the *atabeg* Anur asked Mahmud's brother Muhammad, the ruler of Ba'albak, to take over. He did so, but gave Anur almost complete control over the affairs of state. Muhammad Ibn Buri died of a long illness while Zangi was besieging Damascus, provoking a crisis. Anur and the army commanders agreed to install Muhammad's young son Abaq as nominal ruler. Anur, now in overall command in Damascus, offered the King of Jerusalem an alliance against their common enemy, 'Imad al-Din Zangi. The approach of a Frankish force obliged Zangi to pull back and to abandon, a least temporarily, his ambitions against Damascus. Instead, he turned his

attentions towards the crusader County of Edessa. This lay at the western end of the prosperous and urbanized Jazira region, which, known to the ancient Graeco-Roman world as Mesopotamia, lay between the Tigris and Euphrates rivers. There had been several prominent and powerful rulers in this part of the Islamic Middle East, but they were only occasionally able to direct their energies westwards, against the newly established Crusader States.

This situation changed with the rise of Zangi. The 'Abbasid caliphs had been under Saljuq Turkish domination since 1055 and the current caliph al-Mustarshid had hoped the internal problems of the Great Saljuq Sultanate would enable him to regain real rather than nominal power. His bid failed, but the Turkish commander who defeated him proved to be as skilled diplomatically as he was militarily. This was 'Imad al-Din Zangi, a Turkish officer who, in 1127, took over as *atabeg* in Mosul and northern Iraq. For the

The conquest of most of the Middle East by the Saljuq Turks installed a new ruling and military elite, members of which are portrayed in late 12th- or early 13th-century stucco statuettes from Iran. (Victoria and Albert Museum, London; author's photograph)

next few years Zangi took over city after city but in 1132 he backed the wrong side in a Great Saljuq civil war and suffered one of his few defeats near Samarra in central Iraq. In fact only the support of the Kurdish governor of nearby Tikrit enabled Zangi to avoided capture. This governor was Najm al-Din Ayyub, the father of Saladin (Salah al-Din Yusuf Ibn Ayyub) who was born in Tikrit six years later. Thereafter Zangi was much more cautious in Syria, observing the invading army of the Byzantine Emperor John but avoiding a direct confrontation and then, immediately after the Byzantines withdrew, winning control of the strategic city of Hims by a marriage alliance with Damascus in June 1138. His next campaigns were against fellow Muslims, but in 1144 Zangi turned his attention to the major crusader city of Edessa.

Events in another neighbouring region, Anatolia or what is now Turkey, would have an important bearing upon the forthcoming crusade. It was not until 1134 that the city of Konya became the official capital of the Turkish Saljuq Sultanate of Rum in a move that seemed to reflect important changes in the character of the state. The Saljuq Sultanate of Rum had survived several periods of crisis, not least the devastating passage of the First Crusade at the end of the 11th century. On each occasion it had come back stronger than before, not only militarily but economically and culturally. The longest reigning and most important Saljuq Anatolian ruler of this period was undoubtedly Mas'ud I Ibn Qilij Arslan (1116–56). Having reimposed his authority on the Saljuqs of Rum, he tried to maintain good relations with the

Byzantine Empire whose territory almost surrounded the Saljuqs of Rum to the north, west and south. Instead he took advantage of the decline and fragmentation of his fellow-Muslim, fellow-Turkish Danishmandid neighbours to the east. Mas'ud similarly expanded his territory south-east towards Syria, but in 1146 the Byzantine Emperor Manuel invaded the Saljuq Sultanate in an attempt to regain territory that had been lost over half a century earlier.

The Byzantine recovery of substantial parts of Anatolia had started even before the First Crusade, and involved campaigns against Armenian Christians as well as Muslim Turks. In 1137 Emperor John defeated the local Armenian leader. The following year he moved against the Muslim rulers of northern Syria and besieged the fortress of Shayzar which, under the Banu Munqidh clan, was an Arab-ruled enclave surrounded by Turkish dynasties, Crusader States and, within a few years, by the Isma'ili 'Assassin' mini-state around Masyaf. In the early 1140s Emperor John attempted to take crusader Antioch, and he was still campaigning in neighbouring Cilicia when he died suddenly in April 1143, to be succeeded by his equally warlike son Manuel.

As part of its programme of reconquest the Byzantine Empire had constructed fortresses, some of them massive, to consolidate regained territory and to serve as bases for further campaigns. Several such outposts would feature prominently during the Second Crusade. Although these Byzantine campaigns enabled the Second Crusade to march through western Anatolia, the crusader armies were still exposed to Turkish attack because the Byzantine defensive structure could never seal the new frontier. Similarly, much of the regained territory remained severely depopulated as a result of conquests, reconquests, raids, counter-raids and invasions, not really recovering until the Turkish conquests were completed in the 14th century.

While the Saljuq Sultanate of Rum flourished, the Fatimid Caliphate in Egypt was in gradual but pronounced decline. Here the caliphs of Cairo were Shi'a, as opposed to the 'Abbasid caliphs of Baghdad who were Sunni. Fatimid decline had been halted and for a while reversed under the rule of the *wazirs* ('first ministers') and army commanders of Armenian origin, converts to Islam who wielded power in the name of virtually powerless caliphs. However, things began to fall apart again with the assassination of the *wazir* al-Afdal in 1121, which was followed by a period of political and military confusion, capped by the loss of Tyre to the crusader Kingdom of Jerusalem. As a result, the Fatimids were unable to have much influence upon the course of events in Damascus. Instead, what remained of Fatimid military capability was tied up in the defence of the Caliphate's last outpost in Palestine, the fortified southern port-city of Ascalon.

While the Second Crusade was prompted by events in the Middle East, the way in which the campaign developed was strongly influenced by circumstances within Western, Latin Catholic, Europe. The papacy in Rome was, for example, going through one of its periods of disarray with two prelates being recognized as rival popes by different European rulers. The 'official' Pope, Innocent III, had offered spiritual rewards known as crusading indulgences to those who fought on his behalf against the Norman rulers of southern Italy and Sicily, who were in turn spiritually supported by the rival or 'anti-Pope' Anacletus. Meanwhile, a disputed succession led to civil war in England between the supporters of Stephen and Matilda, which would continue until 1154, gravely inhibiting English participation in the Second Crusade.

The Graeco-Roman temple complex at Ba'albak in Lebanon had been used as a refuge and citadel for centuries. It was also still being used as a local government centre or palace. (Author's photograph)

The existence of two rival Popes was also of concern in Germany where the Western Emperor had a special responsibility for defending and supporting the papacy. As a result Konrad III (king though never officially crowned emperor, and future leader of the Second Crusade) was the 'Roman' Pope's chief supporter against King Roger II of Sicily and the 'anti-Popes'. For the secular and the ecclesiastical elite of Germany, relations between the empire and the papacy had long been of major concern. The ideological debate that had developed between the emperor and Pope in the 11th century had resulted in an arrangement in which the power and authority of both were accepted as being ordained by God. There were nevertheless tensions, not least because the traditional protective power of the emperors over the papacy had been challenged by the papal reform movements of the late 11th and early 12th centuries. At the same time there was increasing acceptance of the theoretical notion of 'Roman imperial authority' having been inherited by the kings of Germany, and of a system of Roman Law which seemed to offer the emperor almost unlimited power. As a result, mid-12th-century German rulers began to use the phrase *sacrum imperium* or 'Holy Empire' in order to have the same status as the Byzantine Empire when dealing with the papacy.

By this time France was already seen as the powerhouse of the crusading movement, both culturally and militarily, so it is not surprising that embassies and letters from the Crusader States, asking for support after the fall of Edessa, were sent to King Louis VII as well as to the Pope and emperor. A letter from Queen Melisende to the Pope had particular impact, while Count Raymond of Tripoli sent envoys directly to King Louis, asking France to mount an expedition to save his principality. The year 1145 also saw the new Pope, Eugenius III, proclaiming what would be the first surviving papal bull or pronouncement calling for a crusade. Designed to be easily understood when read out loud at public gatherings, it offered remission of sins and stated that those who died on their way to the Holy Land were to be considered martyrs who would therefore find a place in heaven alongside those who fell in battle in the Holy Land. Preaching of the new crusade gathered pace during a great meeting at Vézelay in central France during Easter 1146, this task having been delegated to Abbot Bernard of Clairvaux, the finest preacher of the day. His passionate oratory and the promises in the papal bull certainly had an impact, with huge numbers of people promising to go on crusade. However, Bernard was not alone in preaching the new crusade. A renegade Cistercian monk named Ralph was similarly at work. Unfortunately his words took on a violently anti-Jewish tone, resulting in pogroms in northern France and the Rhineland region of Germany, which are now sometimes referred to as the First Holocaust.

From August 1146 until March 1147 Bernard of Clairvaux preached the crusade in Germany and as a result King Konrad III 'took the cross'. Bernard was similarly energetic in his condemnation of the persecution of Jews whipped up by the monk Ralph. In Italy the merchant republics' enthusiasm for crusades was still strong, and as a result the Genoese committed themselves to very expensive campaigns against the Islamic ports of Almeria and Tortosa in what is now Spain. Of course these, if successful, would also bring the Italian merchant cities huge commercial benefits. There was similarly a substantial amount of commercial self-interest amongst those English, Flemish and German Rhineland volunteers for the naval crusade that eventually conquered Lisbon.

Political tensions within some other European kingdoms had other impacts on the course of the Second Crusade. For example, in 1146 Boris, a claimant to the Hungarian throne currently occupied by King Geza, crossed the frontier from the German Empire accompanied by a contingent of *ministerial* knights supplied by the ruler of neighbouring Austria, to seize Pressburg (now Bratislava in Slovakia). The invasion failed but King Geza blamed both the Duke of Bavaria and King Konrad for supporting Boris. So, the approach of Konrad with a huge crusader army the following year worried Geza considerably. The Hungarian king agreed a hurried truce with the German king and ensured that the crusaders' passage across his country went as smoothly as possible.

Away to the east the Byzantine Empire had recently suffered a serious setback during an attempted invasion of the Saljuq Sultanate of Rum, while Armenian rebels were siezing ever more territory in Cilicia. Thus, the Byzantines may have been militarily weakened in Anatolia – a matter that would have a profound impact upon the crusaders' forthcoming efforts to march across this area. Furthermore, like his grandfather Alexius who had to deal with the First Crusade, the Byzantine Emperor Manuel could not be entirely sure what these western Christian forces would do, so, while making peace with the Saljuq Turks, Manuel gave the crusaders the impression that he wanted to take part in their campaign. He had a narrow path to tread.

CHRONOLOGY

1119 Armies of the crusader states defeated at the battle of the Field of Blood.

1121 Assassination of al-Afdal, *wazir* of the Fatimid Caliphate of Egypt.

1122 Count Jocelin of Edessa captured by Turks; death of Turkish Muslim leader Il-Ghazi Ibn Artuq, succeeded by Temür Tash Husam al-Din as Artuqid ruler.

1123 King Baldwin II of Jerusalem captured, held in Harput in eastern Anatolia; death of Sultan Shah Ibn Ridwan, the Saljuq ruler of Syria; *atabeg* Tughtakin becomes the Burid ruler of Damascus.

1124 King Baldwin II of Jerusalem released from Harput (June); nominally Fatimid port-city of Tyre falls to the crusader Kingdom of Jerusalem (July).

1125 Turkish army under Aqsunqur al-Bursuqi defeated by King Baldwin II of Jerusalem at Battle of Azaz; assassination of Aqsunqur al-Bursuqi.

1126 Bohemond II becomes ruler of the Principality of Antioch.

1127 'Imad al-Din Zangi appointed governor of Mosul, seizes Nisibin, Sinjar and Harran in the Jazira region (northern Mesopotamia).

1128 Departure of an unnumbered crusade; death of Tughtigin of Damascus, succeeded by Buri Ibn Tughtigin; 'Imad al-Din Zangi takes Aleppo.

1129 Fulk of Anjou marries Melisende, heiress to the throne of Jerusalem; crusaders unsuccessfully attack Damascus.

1130 Death of Bohemond II of Antioch in battle with Danishmandid Turks; his widow Alice refuses to submit to her father, King Baldwin II of Jerusalem, and asks 'Imad al-Din Zangi for support; 'Imad al-Din defeats alliance of crusader states and Artuqid Turks, takes Mardin in south-eastern Anatolia and Atharib in northern Syria.

1131 Death of King Baldwin II of Jerusalem; Fulk of Anjou becomes king with Melisende as his queen; death of Count Jocelin (of Courtenay) of Edessa; death of Saljuq Sultan Mahmud II results in civil wars in the Great Saljuq Sultanate (Iraq and western Iran).

1132 Isma'il Ibn Buri becomes Burid ruler of Damascus; 'Abbasid Caliph al-Mustarshid defeats 'Imad al-Din Zangi near Samarra.

1134 Konya becomes capital of the Saljuq Turkish Sultanate of Rum (Anatolia); death of Amir Ghazi, the Danishmandid ruler of eastern Anatolia, succeeded by Muhammad Ibn Amir Ghazi.

1135 Mahmud Ibn Buri becomes Burid ruler of Damascus; 'Imad al-Din Zangi of Mosul siezes Kafr Tab, Ma'arat al-Nu'man and Atharib in Syria but fails to take Damascus; disputed succession and civil war between supporters of Stephen and Matilda in England.

1136 Raymond of Poitiers marries Constance and becomes ruler of Antioch.

1137 Byzantine Emperor John Comnenus defeats Armenian ruler Leo the Roupenian in Cilicia, and reaches Antioch; 'Imad al-Din Zangi takes Montferrand from crusaders; death of Count Pons, Raymond II becomes Count of Tripoli.

1138 Emperor John Comnenus campaigns against Muslim rulers of northern Syria; 'Imad al-Din Zangi avoids battle with Byzantine army but gains control of Hims by marriage alliance.

1139 Muhammad Ibn Buri becomes Burid ruler of Damascus; Emperor John campaigns against Danishmandid Turkish ruler of eastern Anatolia; 'Imad al-Din Zangi siezes Ba'albak in Lebanon but fails to take Damascus.

1140 King Fulk of Jerusalem confronts 'Imad al-Din Zangi near Dara'a in southern Syria; Abaq Ibn Muhammad becomes Burid ruler of Damascus; earthquake in Damascus area causes widespread damage (June).

1142 'Imad al-Din Zangi continues campaign against Kurds in south-eastern Anatolia (since 1141); fragmentation of the Danishmandid state in eastern Anatolia; fragmentation of Mengujekid Turkish state in northern Anatolia; Byzantine Emperor John Comnenus fails to take Antioch.

1143 Emperor John Comnenus dies while campaigning in Cilicia, succeeded by his son Manuel; King Fulk of Jerusalem killed in Acre, succeeded by the child King Baldwin III.

1144 'Imad al-Din Zangi conquers Edessa (Urfa) and the eastern half of the crusader County of Edessa; Qara Arslan Fakhr al-Din becomes Artuqid ruler of Hisn Kayfa region of south-eastern Anatolia.

1145 Armenian rebels in Cilicia defeated by Byzantines; Count Raymond of Antioch accepts the suzerainty of the Byzantine Empire; Eugenius II becomes Pope of Rome and proclaims the Second Crusade.

1146 St Bernard of Clairvaux preaches the crusade; persecution of Jews in the Rhineland; assassination of 'Imad al-Din Zangi, succeeded by Sayf al-Din Ghazi I Ibn Zangi in Mosul; *atabeg* Anur of Damascus seizes control of Ba'albak, makes truce with governors of Hims and Hama; King Konrad III of Germany agrees to participate in Second Crusade; unsuccessful invasion of Saljuq Sultanate of Rum by Emperor Manuel.

1147 Nur al-Din Mahmud Ibn Zangi becomes ruler of Aleppo; *atabeg* Anur of Damascus and Nur al-Din of Aleppo agree treaty, sealed by marriage of Nur al-Din to Anur's daughter; governor of Hawran region offers to hand over Busra and Salkhad to the Kingdom of Jerusalem (May-June); King Baldwin III invades Damascus territory; Anur appeals to Nur al-Din for help; together they retake Busra and Salkhad while army of the crusader kingdom withdraws; Pope extends Second Crusade to the Iberian peninsula; Portuguese capture Santarem (March); Pope authorizes a German crusade against the pagan Wends (13 April); first naval contingent of Second Crusade departs from Dartmouth (late May); first land contingents of Second Crusade begin overland march towards the Middle East (May–June); Pope Eugenius and Bernard of Clairvaux preside over ceremony at the Abbey of Saint-Denis to mark the departure of King Louis VII; German and Scandinavian campaigns against Wends (July–September); German crusaders under Konrad III reach Constantinople (10 September); French crusaders under Louis VII reach Constantinople (4–5 October); German forces divide, with Konrad leading the main force towards Saljuq territory (mid-October); crusaders take port-city of Almeria in Iberian peninsula (17 October); Portuguese and northern European crusading fleet conquers Lisbon (24 October); German crusaders under Konrad III defeated by the Saljuq Turks south of Dorylaeum (25 October); Konrad and German crusaders join forces with King Louis; French and German crusaders march along coast and spend Christmas at Ephesus; Normans of southern Italy attack Byzantine Empire in southern Greece.

1148

French crusaders under Louis VII defeat Turkish ambush next to river Meander (1 January) but are then badly mauled as they cross the Honaz Dagi mountains (around 8 January) before reaching Antalya (20 January); crusader fleet sets sail from Lisbon for the Middle East (1 February); Konrad III and German crusaders sail from Constantinople to Acre (arriving April); Louis and French crusaders sail from Antalya to Antioch (arriving 19 March); southern French crusader fleet under Count Alphonse-Jordan of Toulouse reaches Acre (spring); Alphonse-Jordan dies at Caesarea; King Alfonso of León and Castile unsuccessfully attacks Jaen (April);

atabeg Anur of Damascus appeals to Sayf al-Din of Mosul who brings his army to join that of Nur al-Din at Hims; crusader council at Palmarea decides to attack Damascus (June); crusader army reaches outskirts of Damascus (24 July); Damascus army tries to stop crusaders crossing the Barada River but are pushed back; siege of Damascus by Second Crusade (24–28 July); crusaders abandon siege of Damascus and return to the Kingdom of Jerusalem (29 July); King Konrad III sails from Acre (8 September) to Thessalonika and forms an alliance with Emperor Manuel against King Roger of Sicily who has invaded Byzantine territory; most French crusader leaders return to France (autumn) though Louis and Eleanor remain; Genoese and Count of Barcelona conquer Tortosa (30 December); Kingdom of Aragon conquers the lower Ebro plain (1148–49).

1149

Konrad III returns to Germany (spring); King Louis sails from Acre (late April) by ship; Prince Raymond of Antioch killed in battle at 'Ain Murad (29 June); Louis and Eleanor reach Sicily (late July); death of Mu'in al-Din Anur, the *atabeg* of Damascus (28 August); death of Sayf al-Din of Mosul, succeeded by Mawdud Qutb al-Din Ibn Zangi; Louis and Eleanor return to France (November).

1151

Nur al-Din of Aleppo conquers the last fortress of the defunct County of Edessa.

1153

Crusader Kingdom of Jerusalem conquers Ascalon, the last Fatimid stronghold in Palestine.

1154

Nur al-Din takes control of Damascus.

OPPOSING COMMANDERS

CHRISTIAN COMMANDERS

The most obvious difference in the leadership of the First and Second crusades was the involvement of ruling monarchs in the latter expedition. This would remain characteristic of all the main subsequent crusades and resulted from the increased cost of such warfare, the greater administrative efficiency that kings and emperors could provide, and their own increasing ambition.

Konrad III had already been to the Holy Land as a pilgrim and 'guest knight' around 1124 and 1125. He was, in fact, a man of valour, kindly as well as knightly, though also sometimes described as indecisive in politics if not in war. Certainly Konrad was initially reluctant to take the cross, largely because his right to rule the empire was still questioned in several parts of Germany (his enemies tended to refer to him merely as 'King of the Germans'). Born in 1093 or 1094, Konrad was the son of Duke Frederick I of Swabia and of Agnes, a daughter of Emperor Henry IV. As such he was one of the great noblemen of the Staufer faction, rivals of the powerful Welf faction, which similarly claimed the throne. Konrad had, in fact, already made a bid for the crown in 1127 and had for eight years been recognized in parts of Germany as a rival ruler to Emperor Lothar III. Following the latter's death, Konrad was finally elected emperor in March 1138 though once again his unsuccessful rival, Duke Heinrich *Der Stolz* ('the Proud') of Bavaria and Saxony, refused to accept the result and was therefore outlawed.

Nevertheless, Konrad III proved himself a worthy successor to the emperors Henry V and Lothar III as a proponent of imperial renewal and prestige. He also made bold claims to being recognized as the senior ruler throughout Western Europe. Konrad III may indeed have picked up further 'imperial' ideas while in the Byzantine capital during the Second Crusade, especially where relations between church and state were concerned. Certainly Konrad attempted to resist Papal interference later in his reign. His health had, however, been undermined by the rigours of the Second Crusade. On his deathbed Konrad III passed over his own eight-year-old son Frederick and instead designated his nephew and fellow crusader, Frederick of Swabia, as his royal and imperial successor. Once accepted by Germany's electoral college, the Duke of Swabia went on to become one of the medieval empire's most powerful and successful rulers, Frederick I Barbarossa.

King Louis VII of France was considerably younger than Emperor Konrad, having been born in 1120. He was crowned as co-ruler in the Cathedral of Reims in 1135, but his sick father, Louis VI 'the Fat', died two years later. The

A 13th-century portrait of King Konrad III of Germany who, though generally accepted as emperor, was never crowned as such. (*Kölner Königschronik*, Bibliothèque Royale, Brussels)

early part of Louis VII's long reign was somewhat unstable, with the king being involved in quarrels with powerful feudal vassals, some of whom were as powerful as Louis VII himself.

One of Louis VII's greatest assets was, at least for the first part of his reign, his marriage to Eleanor of Aquitaine, which offered the prospect of Eleanor's vast fiefdom being added to the currently small French royal domain centred upon Paris. In the event, this did not happen because Louis and Eleanor separated. Worse still, the Duchess of Aquitaine then married the Count of Anjou's son Henry – the future King Henry II of England – thus linking Aquitaine with the crown of England and sowing the seeds of the Hundred Years War.

Louis VII himself appears to have been a sensitive, serious and deeply religious man whose almost monk-like piety became the butt of cruel jokes by his high-spirited wife Eleanor. In those early years Louis VII was infatuated with this beautiful, highly intelligent and cultured young woman. This scandalized some at the time, with Bernard of Clairvaux complaining that Eleanor had more influence upon the king than he himself did. Louis and Eleanor went together on the Second Crusade, were at the centre of an obscure scandal at Antioch (covered in more detail later) and eventually returned to France on bad terms. After 15 years of marriage, which produced daughters but no sons, they were formally separated in 1152. Both remarried – Louis in that same year to Constance, daughter of the King of Castile, who died childless in 1160. Within five weeks Louis married Adela of Champagne, who finally provided him with a son and heir. This was the future King Philip Augustus 'the Heaven Given' who became one of the most successful rulers in the long history of France, ascending the throne on Louis VII's death in 1180.

King Baldwin III of Jerusalem was born in 1130, the eldest son of Queen Melisende and King Fulk. Though only a babe in arms when his grandfather Baldwin II died in 1131, the latter had already arranged for sovereignty and power to be shared between his daughter Melisende, her husband (later King) Fulk, and the child Baldwin. As he grew up, he merely gave his name to government actions, but was meanwhile educated in history, law and warfare. Baldwin was still young when Fulk died in 1143 and Queen Melisende became regent. The boy king finally came of age in 1145, but Melisende insisted on continued joint rule. In this she was supported by her younger son Almaric, by the higher clergy of the crusader kingdom and by several great lords. Baldwin, it seems, had the support only of some lesser nobles.

Though Baldwin was probably too young to provide active military leadership at the time of the Second Crusade, he appears to have been a strong exponent of the idea of attacking Damascus. After that campaign failed, the power struggle continued in Jerusalem; matters eventually came to a head in 1152 when Melisende was finally forced to give up her formal role in government. Despite the disastrous attack on Damascus, chroniclers and more recent historians have generally seen Baldwin III as the greatest of the crusader kings of Jerusalem, whereas successors were regarded as ruling a state that was in inexorable decline.

MUSLIM COMMANDERS

Chroniclers and historians of the Second Crusade have exaggerated the role of the Zangid rulers, Nur al-Din of Aleppo and Sayf al-Din of Mosul, in the defeat of the Second Crusade. The Muslim commander who really defeated the crusaders was Mu'in al-Din Anur, *atabeg* of Damascus from 1138 until 1149. He remains one of the neglected heroes of the Islamic counter-crusades.

Mu'in al-Din Abu Mansur Anur, whose name meant 'Anur, Supporter of the Faith, Father of Mansur', had been a *mamluk* or *ghulam* slave-recruited soldier of Turkish or Turkoman origin. Having received training, he was released and then entered the service of Tughtigin, the Turkish *atabeg* or 'father-figure adviser' of a Saljuq prince who ruled Damascus. Tughtigin himself effectively ruled the principality from 1104 until his death in 1128, establishing an originally *atabeg* dynasty known, rather confusingly, after Tughtigin's son Buri (Böri in Turkish) as the Burids. It ruled a substantial part of what are now southern Syria, eastern Lebanon and Jordan until

TOP, LEFT
The carved ivory cover of Queen Melisende of Jerusalem's *Psalter* is believed to have been made in the Kingdom of Jerusalem during the first half of the 12th century. Its style mixes Western European, particularly southern Italian, and Byzantine elements. (British Museum, London)

TOP, RIGHT
One of very few buildings that can be specifically credited to the *atabeg* Mu'in al-Din Anur of Damascus is this tower. It was added to the outside of the massive Roman theatre at Busra in 502 AH (AD 1147–48). (C. Yovitchitch photograph)

1154, though its later representatives rarely held the real reins of power, themselves being dominated by *atabegs*.

Anur came to power through a coup on 29 April 1138, though he never became the titular ruler of the state. Instead Anur was content to be recognized as the *Isfahsalar* or senior army commander and *atabeg* under nominal rulers of the originally *atabeg* Burid dynasty, who were by now usually called princes. Anur was, in fact, *atabeg* in the name of three successive Burid princes: Mahmud Ibn Buri until 1139, Muhammad Ibn Buri until 1140, and Abaq Ibn Muhammad until Anur's own death.

Anur's overriding priority was to preserve the independence of the Damascene state, and to do so he often cooperated with the neighbouring crusader Kingdom of Jerusalem. Even when the traditional alliance between Damascus and Jerusalem was broken by the Second Crusade, Anur restrained his troops from inflicting too much damage on their defeated foes and then succeeded in returning to his policy of maintaining a balance of power between the crusader 'Franks' to the west and the Zangid rulers, Nur al-Din and Sayf al-Din, to the north. Only with Anur's death on 28 August 1149, from liver failure or dysentery, did this policy collapse, resulting in Nur al-Din Ibn Zangi's takeover of Damascus six years later. Anur was buried in or next to a small palace inside the Citadel of Damascus where he had lived, but sadly its precise location remains unknown.

The later medieval Suq al-Atarin covered market in Aleppo, the wealthy city from which Nur al-Din continued his father Zangi's work of rolling back the crusader conquests. (Author's photograph)

In addition to being a skilled soldier, politician and diplomat, Anur was a friend and patron of scholars and poets, one of the best-known being the Arab soldier, politician, diplomat and scholar Usama Ibn Munqidh. It is from Usama that we know that Anur was not only highly cultured but had a well developed – although, by modern standards, rather rough – sense of humour. This was shown in a story concerning a pet lion that had been raised in Damascus. According to Usama Ibn Munqidh, Anur one day asked for the animal to be brought into the courtyard of his palace:

> Then he said to the master of his table, 'Bring out a sheep from among the animals being prepared for slaughter for the kitchen and leave it in the inner courtyard so that we may see how the lion annihilates it' … As soon as the sheep saw the lion, whose trainer had set it free from the chain which was around its neck, [the sheep] rushed to it and butted it. The lion took to flight and began to circle around the pool with the sheep following behind, chasing and butting it. We were all overcome with laughter. Anur regarded this cowardly lion as being an ill omen and ordered it to be killed. As for the sheep, it was exempted from ever being slaughtered. (Usamah Ibn Munqidh, 1927; 137)

Abu Sa'id Mujir al-Din Abaq Ibn Muhammad was the titular ruler of Damascus at the time of the Second Crusade. Dismissed by the crusader chronicler William of Tyre as 'indolent by nature', Abaq was actually more active than his immediate predecessors. He clearly had no wish to be merely the nominal ruler of Damascus, though in the end his ambition to regain real authority for the Burid dynasty led to its disappearance. Though he came to the throne in 1140, Abaq had virtually no power until the death of his formidable *atabeg* Anur in 1149. Five years later Mujir al-Din Abaq was forced to hand his capital over to Nur al-Din. In return he was allocated an *'iqta* or fief at Hims in central Syria. Unfortunately he could not accept defeat and tried to stir up a revolt against the new regime in Damascus. When this failed, Nur al-Din exiled Abaq to the little town of Balis overlooking the Euphrates. From here Mujir al-Din Abaq soon went into voluntary exile in Baghdad, where he lived until his death in 1169.

Mahmud Ibn Zangi Abu'l-Qasim al-Malik al-'Adil Nur al-Din was the greatest leader of the Islamic counter-crusades before the rise of his own protégé, Saladin. Born in 1118, the second son of 'Imad al-Din Zangi, he took over as ruler in Aleppo shortly after his father was assassinated in 1146. From then until his death in 1174 Nur al-Din united much of the Islamic Middle East against the invading 'Franks' and laid the political, military and cultural foundations upon which Saladin would build. Being the second son, Nur al-Din did not receive the central provinces of his father's realm, which went to his elder brother Sayf al-Din; instead he gained control of the more recently conquered western provinces. These were not only smaller and with fewer resources than those of his brother, but were also more vulnerable. Even Nur al-Din's main city of Aleppo stood dangerously close to the

ABOVE
A copper fils (low value coin) minted for Mawdud Ibn Zangi, the younger brother of Sayf al-Din and Nur al-Din, who became ruler of Mosul shortly after the defeat of the Second Crusade. (Private collection)

LEFT
In the 12th century the fortified old city of Damascus had a number of major roads, between which were narrow streets and culs-de-sac. Many were lined with shops, workshops or private houses, most of which had their own internal courtyards. (Author's photograph)

crusader frontier. Furthermore, his responsibilities as ruler of a frontier zone meant that Nur al-Din shouldered the main burden of waging jihad against the invaders.

During his numerous campaigns, the ruler of Aleppo won victories but also suffered defeats. Most importantly perhaps, he eventually took over Damascus and thus created an almost united front against the crusader states – a situation made even more dangerous for the Franks when the army Nur al-Din sent to Egypt took over that country as well. Here Nur al-Din had little authority because the new governor, Saladin, had ambitions of his own. In fact tensions were rising and Nur al-Din was actually preparing a campaign against Saladin when he fell ill and died on 15 May 1174.

Ghazi Ibn Zangi Sayf al-Din was the eldest son of 'Imad al-Din Zangi, who took over as ruler of a large part of northern Iraq and south-eastern Turkey after his father was murdered in 1146. A third brother, Nusrat al-Din became governor of Harran, between the territories of Sayf al-Din and Nur al-Din, while the youngest brother, Qutb al-Din was as yet too young to have responsibility for a province. Described as generous and renowned for providing his soldiers with large meals both in the morning and evening, Sayf al-Din was also credited with several important military reforms, some of which enabled his elite cavalry to meet heavily armoured crusader knights on equal terms.

Sayf al-Din was a particularly tolerant ruler, especially towards the substantial indigenous Christian communities of northern Iraq. He was also a pious Muslim whose reign saw an upsurge in intellectual life in Mosul, particularly in the construction of *madrasa* religious colleges, which taught not only the Islamic religion but also mathematics and literature. Sayf al-Din's reign was nevertheless short. A year after the Second Crusade he fell ill while campaigning against the rival Artuqid Turkish ruler of Mardin. He died a few weeks later in November 1149 and was buried in the Atabakiya *madrasa*, which he himself had founded in Mosul.

Ma'sud I Ibn Qilich Arslan Rukn al-Din ruled the Saljuq Sultanate of Rum from 1116 to 1156, having succeeded his brother Malik Shah II. The Second Crusade was only one of many dramatic events that arose during his long reign. His father, Qilich Arslan I, had faced and survived the First Crusade, after which he had expanded his ambitions in several directions. Qilich Arslan I's sons initially focused on surviving the near chaos that followed his death, much of it caused by their competition to take over the Saljuq Sultanate of Rum. Ma'sud I Ibn Qilich Arslan emerged the victor, but even so he quarrelled with his Danishmandid father-in-law, was briefly overthrown in 1125 by his brother Arap, fled to Constantinople, formed alliances with the Byzantine emperor and, having patched up his quarrel, with the Danishmandids as well. This enabled Ma'sud to regain his throne after only a short exile, after which he moved his capital to Konya. Ma'sud I Ibn Qilich Arslan's own long reign mostly consisted of quarrels and warfare, yet when he died in 1156 he left the Sultanate of Rum much stronger than it had been when he came to the throne, enabling his successors to make Konya one of the great cultural centres of the medieval Islamic Middle East.

OPPOSING FORCES

Although the armies involved on both sides of this campaign would have appeared very similar to those that had fought during the First Crusade, there had been significant developments during the intervening half-century.

CHRISTIAN FORCES

On the crusader side the forces were larger, better equipped and better organized than those of the First Crusade. Estimating medieval numbers is, of course, notoriously difficult and the Byzantine Emperor Manuel's claim to have counted 900,000 Germans crossing the Bosphorus is clearly a poetic exaggeration. In reality King Konrad could probably have raised a maximum

The cycle of wall paintings in the lower Church of St Clement at Schwarzrheindorf near Bonn was probably painted during the preaching of the Second Crusade or after their patron's return. Here the 'Slaughter of the Wicked' illustrates the long-hafted infantry axes used in 12th-century Germany. (*In situ* Church of St Clement, Schwarzrheindorf; R.T. Wildeman photograph)

'David cutting off Goliath's head'. The arms and armour are typical of early 12th-century France, though the helmet worn without a mail coif may indicate the Philistine giant's alien identity. (*In situ*, nave of the abbey church of La Madeleine, Vézelay; author's photograph)

of 2,000 knights from the German Empire while King Louis could raise a maximum of 700 knights from his own royal domain. His feudal subordinates could have fielded smaller numbers, the particularly wealthy Count of Flanders reportedly being able to raise 600 knights. Meanwhile the Kingdom of Jerusalem could probably have fielded an army of around 550 knights plus some 6,000 infantry. Of course, not all these troops would have been committed to the Second Crusade and it is clear that the numbers that reached the Middle East were substantially smaller than those who had set out. More specifically, the Templars promised some 130 troops during a meeting in Paris in April 1147. This may have been the elite contingent that accompanied King Louis's largely French crusading army on its march overland.

Once the Latin States had been established in the Middle East, the theoretically feudal structure of their 'Frankish' society meant that all able-bodied citizens could be summoned in time of need. This applied whether or not the men were landholders, but in reality the knights were called first, with those of sergeant rank acting as a reserve (La Monte, 1932; 159).

It has been suggested that some of the earliest *turcopoles* within the armies of these crusader states were associated with the mixed Turkish–Greek population of Bythnia in north-western Anatolia through which the First Crusade had marched[1]. Nevertheless, the fact that Middle Eastern *turcopoles* were almost invariably executed as apostates if captured by Muslims strongly suggests that they were converts, forced or otherwise, from Islam to Christianity.

Most of the professional soldiers enlisted by the crusader states were probably recruited locally from amongst Latin settlers, including recently arrived European mercenaries and knightly crusaders who had chosen to remain. The promise of rich fiefs in newly conquered territory had been used to encourage knights, both resident and newcomers, to take part in offensive expeditions beyond the kingdom's frontiers and this was probably also true of the assault upon Damascus.

A great deal is known about the theoretical feudal obligations of the 12th-century Kingdom of Jerusalem and, although this may represent an ideal rather than reality, it may have been relatively accurate for the expansionist first half of the 12th century. Thus, according to law, the king's vassals owed military service for up to a year within the kingdom, and payment was made only for additional time under arms, even to those knights or sergeants who had money fiefs (La Monte; 141–44). The question of what exactly counted as service inside or outside the kingdom was, and remains, a matter of debate. Even in the early days Egypt was agreed to be 'outside' whereas the situation along the open frontiers of Syria was less clear.

Military leadership within the crusades was based upon the same concepts as those in Western Europe. In practice, however, military priorities in the Middle East tended to be more urgent than those in most European states

1 Vryonis, S., 'Byzantine and Turkish Societies and their sources of manpower', in V.J. Parry & M.E. Yapp (eds.), *War, Technology and Society in the Middle East* (London 1975) 133–4.

A large part of what is now eastern France lay within the German Empire during the 12th century. These two foot soldiers, carved around 1130 to 1140, reflect the continuing importance of infantry combat in medieval Germany. (*In situ* abbey church, Andlau; author's photograph)

and as a result the rulers of Jerusalem had even greater concern to retain centralized control over all institutions of government. At the time of the Second Crusade the settler aristocracy of these crusader states was still very powerful and had certainly not entered the decline that would characterize the 13th century. Several of these noble families would also play a leading role in the Second Crusade, and would be widely blamed for its failure.

The dismal results of the Second Crusade may also have been a major factor in an attempt to reform this feudal structure, resulting on the *Assise sur la Ligece* which was drawn up around 1160. Initially it was seen as a victory of the king and the lower knights over the higher barons, but it also weakened and fragmented these higher baronies at a time of increasing military threat. Furthermore, it would result in an increasing reliance upon the Military Orders and hired mercenary troops. Nevertheless, the significance of the Military Orders should not be overstated at the time of the Second Crusade. Military support from some of the indigenous Christian communities was probably more important, including that of the Maronite Christians of Lebanon. As will be seen below, the Muslims of Lebanon would play a similarly important role in the forces of Damascus.

Knowledge and understanding of Islam was barely greater in the Second Crusade than it had been in the First. More surprising, perhaps, was the lack of awareness of the concept of Islamic jihad, which was only later recognized as a form of religious military motivation comparable to the Christian Crusade itself. The reasons why men went on crusade have fascinated historians for generations. Crusades were in many respects armed pilgrimages – pilgrimage having long been the most obvious way for a nobleman to redeem past sins. The warlike nature of a crusade would also have appealed to a feudal nobility whose socio-political purpose was itself military. In Germany, meanwhile, religious fervour was heightened by a widespread feeling that the end of the world was approaching, partly resulting from the perceived decline of a German 'Roman' empire – regarded as the last of the four great world monarchies – whose fall would supposedly be followed by the coming of the Antichrist. Although there was widespread support for the new crusade, it remained unfocussed, and in the end Konrad's expeditionary army was largely drawn from his own power base of southern Germany.

This copy of Albert of Aachen's history of the First Crusade includes an illustration of a crusader with a cross on his shield. It was made in 1140, only a few years before the far less successful Second Crusade. (*Historia Heirosolymitana*, Ms. Lat. 677, f.12r, Preussischer Kulturbesitz, Berlin)

Not all the participants in the Second Crusade were knights, though official designated crusading expeditions tended to consist of clearly defined military contingents mobilized by great lords or rulers and included a large proportion of men of recognized social status. Even so, the main contingents of the Second Crusade were still encumbered by large numbers of poorly disciplined and ill-armed camp followers. Very few made it to the Middle East, and as Odo of Deuil, himself a participant in the Second Crusade, commented, 'the weak and helpless are always a burden to their commanders and a source of prey to their enemies.'

The commanders were aware of the need for discipline and did what they could to enforce it, though with varied success. At Metz, where the main French contingent gathered in mid-June 1147, King Louis proclaimed the 'Laws of the Camp' to which all leaders swore obedience but, as Odo again recalled, they were not always obeyed. One Flemish crusader was punished for stealing money from a Greek money changer and was hanged in full view of the city of Constantinople as a gesture of good faith.

The naval expedition that formed part of the Second Crusade reflected increasing confidence about the maritime situation in both the Mediterranean and the Atlantic. From 1124, when the crusader states had completed their conquest of the Syro-Palestinian coast north of Ascalon, the entire littoral from Constantinople to Jaffa was in Christian hands, along with the island of Cyprus. Equally important for major crusading expeditions were advances in the ability to transport horses by sea.

Sea lanes from western Europe to the Holy Land were now safer, although vessels from the Atlantic still had to pass through the Muslim-dominated Straits of Gibraltar. Ships and even fleets from northern and western Europe had of course passed successfully through the Straits of Gibraltar in previous centuries but none is known to have sailed back out again; nor would any do so for many decades. Instead their crews abandoned or sold their ships and returned home overland (Lewis, 1976).

Despite an overall similarity in equipment and tactics amongst the land forces that took part in the Second Crusade, a number of sources noted differences between the Germans and the French. Whether these were traditional, scholarly concepts or reflected current reality is, however, less clear. For example the Byzantine chronicler John Kinnamos maintained that 'the French are particularly capable of riding horseback in good order and attacking with the spear, and their cavalry surpasses that of the Germans in speed. The Germans, however, are able to fight on foot better than the French and excel in using the great sword' (Kinnamos, 1976). This opinion was echoed by William of Tyre, who noted that King Konrad's German knights dismounted to fight their way across the Barada river outside Damascus and stated that this was 'the custom of the Teutons when they are faced with a crisis in battle'.

French military organization was nevertheless widely seen as the model which other Western European states tried to follow during the 12th century. It was obviously the basis for the organization of Louis VII's contingent on the Second Crusade when the king and his advisers agreed that masses of ill-armed 'poor' were a hindrance to crusading, which should be left to properly equipped and financed professionals. In the event, this view was no more successful in France that it was in Germany, and the French army, like the German, was encumbered by large numbers of non-combatants and civilian pilgrims.

Each crusading army consisted of smaller contingents, most of which were formed around the households of the king, his senior noblemen and churchmen. One of the main such contingents in the French crusading expedition was led by a woman, Eleanor of Aquitaine, who had summoned her own vassals. However, it seems likely that the Byzantine chronicler Nicetas misunderstood what was reported to him when he referred to a force of fully armed Amazons: 'At the head of these was one in particular, richly dressed, that went by the name the Lady of the Golden Boot. Her elegance and her bearing and the freedom of her movements recalled the celebrated leader of the Amazons'. Eleanor, it seems, made an impression wherever she went.

Eleanor's Duchy of Aquitaine had, of course, been the birthplace of troubadour culture in France, from which it would spread across most of Western Europe. One troubadour who is known to have taken part in the Second Crusade was Jaufré Rudel, the Prince of Blaye. He may have gone with his close friend Hugh of Lusignan to hear Bernard of Clairvaux preach at Vézelay, yet it was still the secular and erotic theme of 'love from afar' which dominated his verses, including those in a crusading setting. Rudel's song *Quan lo rossinhols en foillos* (*When the nightingale in the woods*) may even have been composed after his arrival in the Middle East, probably with the contingent of southern French crusaders who landed at Acre in April 1148. Seven of Jaufré Rudel's poems have survived, the best known being *Lanquand li jorn son lonc en mai* (*When the days are long in May*), whose second verse draws together the themes of carnal desire, crusading and the Islamic Middle East:

'Hercules fighting the Hydra,' on a carved bone or ivory English draughts piece, perhaps made in St Albans between 1125 and 1150. (Victorian and Albert Museum, inv. 374-1871, London; author's photograph)

A seal impression of Prior Walter, a senior Hospitaller, from a document drawn up the year of the disastrously unsuccessful crusader siege of Damascus in 1148. (British Museum, London)

Although this Coptic Christian Gospel was made at Damietta in Egypt in 1179–80, its representations of military figures reflect the local militias of much of the Arab Middle East. (Ms. Copte 13, f.83v, Bibliothèque Nationale, Paris)

Never in love shall I rejoice
Unless I enjoy this love from afar,
For nobler or better I do not know
In any direction, near or far,
Her worth is so true and perfect
That there in the kingdom of the Saracens
I would, for her, be proclaimed captive.[2]

This song inspired a later fictionalized account of Jaufré Rudel's participation in the Second Crusade and his death in the Holy Land, including the idea that he fell in love with his unseen amour, Countess Hodierna of Tripoli, because of the descriptions of her beauty given by returning pilgrims.

MUSLIM FORCES

During this period Middle Eastern Islamic armies were rarely or ever as large as their European opponents maintained. In fact the professional forces around which larger armies assembled in times of crisis tended to be remarkably small. On the other hand they often incorporated highly trained, well-equipped and expensively maintained elite units which were sometimes organized in a remarkably modern 'regimental' manner. Even the armies of the Great Saljuq Sultanate, which still ruled most of Iran and Iraq, rarely exceeded 10,000 men, and this was huge when compared to the forces available to the fragmented successor states in Syria.

Central to the system of professional troops was the *'iqta* system of usually territorial fiefs. This had been known before the arrival of the Saljuq Turks, but then increased rapidly in importance under the Great Saljuq Sultans. In contrast to the military and administrative elites maintained by *'iqta* fiefs were the turbulent but nevertheless often highly effective *ahdath* urban militias. These were headed by, or at least partially under the control of, a city's *ra'is*, literally meaning 'head' man who often fulfilled a role comparable to a mayor. In many respects the *ra'is* also served as an intermediary between the indigenous Arabic-speaking population and a largely Turkish ruling or military elite.

2 Switten, M., 'Singing the Second Crusade', in M. Gervers (ed.), *The Second Crusade and the Cistercians* (New York 1992) 71.

Another distinctive feature of Islamic military practice which reflected the sophisticated civilization of the Islamic Middle East was the pigeon post which could provide an extremely fast and generally reliable government or military communications system. By the end of the 11th century many Islamic states were using carrier pigeons as a matter of course, these trained birds being capable of maintaining a flying speed of over 100kph and covering distances of more than 1,500km. It is also clear that Nur al-Din's 'establishment' of a pigeon post throughout Syria in 1171 is misleading, since he probably formalized an existing ad hoc system.

The most distinctive and yet most misunderstood aspect of Islamic military culture during this period was the *ghulam* or *mamluk*, the so-called 'slave soldier'. A closer look at the lives of some of these men shows that they included willing recruits and perhaps even volunteers, though the majority may well have been children or younger prisoners of war, enslaved and sold by their captors. Surviving documentary evidence indicates that the cost of a Turkish adolescent or boy to be trained as a *ghulam* varied during this period but usually seems to have been around 30 *dinars* (moderately high value gold coins) while an individual who showed particular promise as a result of superior strength, athleticism or demonstrated intelligence, could cost much more. In 12th century Syria these prices were roughly comparable to those of horses, which ranged from 20 dinars for an inferior animal to 100 for a good one.

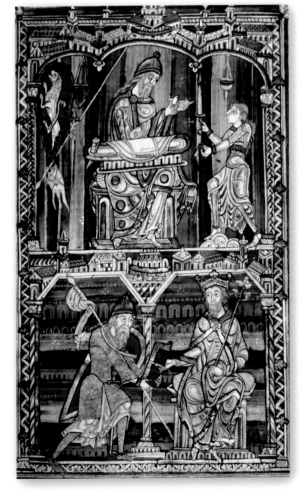

Pliny writing and presenting his book to the Emperor Vespasian in a 12th-century English or northern French manuscript. Pliny appears as a typical knight of the period. (*Naturalis Historia*, Ms. 263, f.10v, Médiathèque Louis-Aragon, Ville du Mans)

The relationships between a patron and his client, and between a master and his slave, in medieval Islam are not widely understood today. In much of the Western world the entire question has been wilfully misinterpreted and used as a stick with which to beat Islamic civilization as a whole. Both relationships were found within a military context and, although they were clearly different, in both cases the senior or dominant person accepted some of the responsibilities of being a 'father' while the junior person accepted those of a 'son'. Following the manumission or freeing of a slave, including *mamluks* or *ghulams* who were legally freed upon completion of their military training and education, the relationship changed, but still retained many of these 'father and son' aspects.

While *mamluks* or *ghulams* formed the military and increasingly also the political elites of Turco-Islamic states in the Middle East, they were clearly not the majority of troops available to local rulers. Free rather than freed soldiers were cheaper to hire and maintain, ranging from highly trained and educated professionals of Turkish, Arab and Kurdish origin, to groups of almost ungovernable tribesmen of comparable origins.

Within the Middle East itself the often only superficially Muslim Turkish tribes, or Turkomans, remained a constant problem for Islamic civilization in Syria during the 11th and 12th centuries. Like the similar Kurdish tribes, they

An episode in the *Shahnamah* epic on a late 12th- or early 13th-century ceramic beaker from Iran. Its military equipment and animal harness reflect that of the Saljuq Turkish military classes that dominated Syria and Anatolia as well as Iran. (Inv. 28.2, Freer Gallery, Washington; author's photographs)

were often ready to fight for any lord but remained very difficult for rulers to control. A telling description of them comes from the pen of the 12th-century Damascus chronicler Ibn al-Qalanisi:

> They gathered from every quarter, and every direction in vast numbers and manifested strength as lions seeking their prey and gyrfalcons hovering over their victims.

The motivations of the urban *ahdath* militias were very different, though their religious passions could be turned against differing Islamic sects as well as against invading Christian crusaders. To a large degree these militias resulted from the militarization of northern Syria, and especially of its cities, in the period immediately prior to the First Crusade. A comparable militarization of southern Syrian cities including Damascus itself developed during the first half of the 12th century in the face of crusader aggression. This was closely associated with a revival or reinvention of the concept of jihad, which nevertheless remained a largely Sunni rather than Shi'a Muslim phenomenon.

Islam was, of course, important to those involved in warfare, even when there was no specific call to jihad, just as Christianity was to the crusaders. The presence of religious figures in battle similarly went back to the days of the Prophet Muhammad himself, and by the 12th century they included a recognized class of Islamic religious scholars. One of their number emerged as a hero of the defence of Damascus against the Second Crusade, namely Hujjat al-Din Yusuf Ibn Dirbas al-Fandalawi al-Maghribi. Another less orthodox Muslim religious group involved in warfare against the crusaders was the sufis or mystics. Their presence as an organized group seems to have been a recent phenomenon in Syria. It had also resulted in the building of *khanqahs* or buildings for members of a specific sufi fraternity, at least one of which would be mentioned during the siege of Damascus in 1148.

Despite the importance of religion, Muslim military forces clearly included men – and indeed leaders – who did not live their lives according to strict Islamic rules. 'Imad al-Din Zangi was, for example, renowned for his tendency to get drunk. Though he was a Turk whose way of life remained close to that of his pre-Islamic Central Asian forebears, the place of wine in Arab society is perhaps more significant since this community formed the very heart of medieval Islamic culture. It might also explain the presence of so many vineyards in Syria at the time of the Second Crusade.

Another misleading tendency amongst historians of the Crusades has been to focus too much upon the tactics and equipment of Turkish or Turkoman tribal troops. Their horse-archery harassment traditions were undoubtedly dramatic and often effective, yet they were still only part of the military picture. Indeed their significance had declined by the mid-12th century, at least within the Middle Eastern heartlands of medieval Islamic civilization. A more accurate impression of the reality of warfare in these regions can be found in a Persian poem written for a newly dominant Turkish ruling and military elite a decade or so after the siege of Damascus. The *Warqa wa Gulshah* is a love story set amid the warlike adventures of nominally Arab tribes whose style of warfare are nevertheless those of the 12th-century Turco-Islamic elite:

> Of their lances, greedy for slaughter, to the heads made ardent
> Of their javelins they dazzled the eyes …
> The whistling of the arrows and the smack of the bows
> The blows of maces and the tearing of lances.[3]

Describing individual combat between heroes, the poet wrote:

> Warqa quickly seized his lance, bravely he took it to the field of battle.
> With his lance he charged against them, the Arab horseman Warqa with the courage of a lion,
> He struck with his lance a brave pursuer of the armies, the heart filled with hatred, he struck with his arm.
> He pinned the two arms to his sides. When he received this blow his heart caught fire.
> Once again he urged on his horse like a she-wolf. Next he shouted very loudly.[4]

A few years after the Second Crusade the Egyptian scholar al-Tarsusi wrote his famous military textbook for Saladin. Virtually all of its content was based upon the military technology, tactics and traditions of the previous Fatimid dynasty which were in turn a direct development of those of the earlier 'Abbasid Caliphate. As such, al-Tarsusi's work may provide a picture of the military reality in mid-12th-century Damascus. The emphasis on archery in

The few fragments of wall painting that survive from the Islamic Middle East during this period show that their style was similar to that in illustrated manuscripts or decorated ceramics. (Metropolitan Museum of Art, inv. Pulitzer.52.20.1, New York; author's photograph)

3 Ayyuqi, (ed. & tr. A.S. Melikian-Chirvani), 'Le Roman de Varqe et Golsâh', *Arts Asiatiques*, 22 (1970) lines 328–331.
4 Ayyuqi, op. cit., lines 1143–47.

TOP, LEFT
The mid-12th-century wall paintings at Schwarzrheindorf include battles between Virtues and Vices, where the former appear as typical German knights and the latter have long Middle Eastern robes and beards. (*In situ* Church of St Clement, Schwarzrheindorf; M. Kranz photograph)

TOP, RIGHT
This 12th-century glazed ceramic bottle stopper found at Raqqa in north-eastern Syria represents a soldier of this period with a conical helmet and a round shield. (Museum für Islamische Kunst, Berlin)

BOTTOM
Judas Maccabeus and knights jousting in an early 12th-century French illustrated Bible. (*Dijon Bible*, Ms.2, f.380v, Bibliothèque Municipale, Dijon)

al-Tarsusi's work is particularly interesting as it is based upon an Arab, pre-Turkish, tradition of infantry archery. As such we can imagine the defenders of Damascus in 1148 following his advice that 'If you are shooting from above a wall, hold the bow horizontally' (Tarsusi, 1968; 146). Al-Tarsusi also describes a number of crossbows ranging from large siege weapons to the small hand-held weapons that were almost certainly used against the besiegers of Damascus (Tarsusi, 1968; 132–33 and 110–12).

Then there was the question of military training within a civilization whose armies had been substantially professional for centuries. By the mid-12th century most Middle Eastern Islamic cities had a *maydan* or designated training ground close by. Damascus may have been unusual in having two such *maydans*, the 'Green' or grassy and the 'Stoney', both of which would feature in the forthcoming siege. In most respects, however, the military structures and personnel of the mid-12th-century *amirate* of Damascus was normal for that part of the Middle East. Turkish speakers enlisted as regulars tended to be known as Turks while the temporary volunteers who often arrived in substantial groups were called Turkomans (Zanki, 1989; 261–62). The former formed over three-quarters of the Damascene standing army and lived inside the walled city, its immediately neighbouring suburbs or as garrisons in other fortified places. Meanwhile the volunteers usually lived in surrounding districts (Zanki, 1989; 264), either in villages or in their own tented encampments.

The resulting army of Damascus which defeated the Second Crusade consisted of six main elements distinguished by the nature of their service as well as their origins (Zanki, 1989; 253–54). The most important was the ruler's *'askar* or small corps of full-time regular soldiers. Of much lower status but perhaps equal military importance when facing the Second Crusade was the *ahdath* or militia of Damascus, most of whom seem to have been drawn from the ranks of the urban poor (Zanki, 1989; 265), supposedly maintaining order but sometimes also being a source of trouble themselves. Then there were the Turkoman and Kurdish volunteers, plus Arab bedouin who were more like regional allies.

The local *mutatawiy'a* volunteers were more like a military reserve than the religiously motivated *jihadi* volunteers. They could be summoned when required and mostly seem to have been refugees from territory lost to crusader occupation. Another group was called *al-haramiyya*, 'the robbers', who used their local knowledge to harrass enemy supply routes (Zanki, 1989; 273–77). Armenian soldiers were similarly present in this part of Syria, though in smaller numbers than in the north or in Egypt. For example Altuntash, the rebel commander of the Hawran region in 1147, was a Turkified Armenian convert (Dédéyan, 2001).

The rulers of Damascus could also call upon military support from feudal subordinates, including those from the Lebanon who played such a vital role in 1148. Precisely where those archers 'from the Biqa'a' Valley came from is unclear. However, a collection of local accounts made by Tannus al-Shidyaq in the 19th century included a document dating from 1147 when Mujir al-Din Abaq, nominal ruler of Damascus, issued an edict confirming the *'iqta* fief held by an *amir* named Nahid al-Dawla Abu'l-Asha'ir Buhtur of the Arslanid clan. This he held in return for maintaining local order and recognizing the authority of Damascus (Salibi, 1959; 189–96).

Perseus with the Gorgon's head in a copy of the 'Book of Stars' by al-Sufi, made in 525 AH (AD 1130–31). The hero is shown in 12th-century Arab costume, wielding the straight sword that was standard Arab if not Turkish military equipment. (*Kitab al-Sufar*, Ms. Ahmed III 3493, f.30r, Topkapi Museum, Istanbul)

OPPOSING PLANS

CHRISTIAN PLANS

Unlike their predecessors in the First Crusade, the leaders of the Second Crusade had a reasonably accurate idea of the distance, terrain, climatic factors and foes that they would be facing. On the other hand, the plans for such a long-term, long-distance campaign had to remain flexible, not least because circumstances could – and did – change between the mustering of forces and their arrival in the Middle East. Furthermore, communications were so slow that it could take a year for an officially sanctioned report or document to get from Jerusalem to the courts of Western Europe. Rumour, of course, flew faster and was greatly feared by those trying to control events. Popular enthusiasm was almost as uncontrollable as rumour at a time when those in authority had limited real power, and as a result the church had little choice but to bow to popular pressure, eventually sanctioning 'crusading' campaigns in the Baltic, the Iberian peninsula and North Africa. Meanwhile, the papacy tried to keep senior secular leaders focused upon the Middle East where the initial plan had been to regain the city and County of Edessa.

The agricultural surroundings of Damascus as they were in the late 19th century. (Ex-J.H. Vincent and J.W. Lee, *Earthly Steps of the Man of Galilee*, New York, 1894)

Some planners of the Second Crusade, including the Pope, consciously used the First Crusade as a model and attempted to improve upon it. However, King Louis VII's dismissal of King Roger of Sicily's suggestion that part of the French contingent travel through southern Italy before crossing the Adriatic to Byzantine territory probably reflected his awareness of the tensions between Roger and Emperor Manuel. Consequently, Louis followed the Danube through Germany, Hungary then across the Byzantine Balkans – a route that Konrad III of Germany had already decided upon. In the event, King Konrad's army was able to move faster than the main contingent of the First Crusade had done because of much better preparation, a last-minute re-establishment of good relations with Hungary, the gathering of a fleet of transport ships to carry supplies along the Danube and the carrying of prefabricated wooden bridges. It was a remarkable achievement for armies that were much bigger than their predecessors in the First Crusade.

A comparable degree of planning was needed by the maritime contingents. By the mid-12th century there was considerable knowledge of naval routes through the Straits of Gibraltar. Not only had a northern fleet passed through the Straits as part of the First Crusade, but more recently Norwegian ships had attacked the Andalusian coast and the Balearic Islands – events which would have given confidence to the Second Crusade's Atlantic fleet of 1147.

While part of the Atlantic maritime expedition, having helped conquer Lisbon, continued its planned journey to the Holy Land across the Mediterranean, the main land contingents continued with their original plans by setting off across Anatolia. Konrad III apparently still saw Edessa as his ultimate destination, but in Syria itself strategic priorities were already changing. While the Count of Edessa obviously wanted to regain his lost

TOP, LEFT
When faced with the massive army of the Second Crusade, the Muslim population of Damascus flocked to the city's 8th-century Great Mosque where one of Islam's most sacred relics, the Koran of the Caliph 'Uthman, was held, and was brought out to raise the people's morale. (Author's photograph)

TOP, RIGHT
The broken Jewish gravestone of a 'daughter of Isaac, drowned in Sanctification of the Oneness of God in the year 906 on Friday the 5th of Iyar' (1146), a victim of an anti-Jewish pogrom carried out in Mainz during the preaching of the Second Crusade. (E.L. Rapp)

Campaigns and movements in the Middle East 1146–May 1148 (frontiers *c.* 1147)

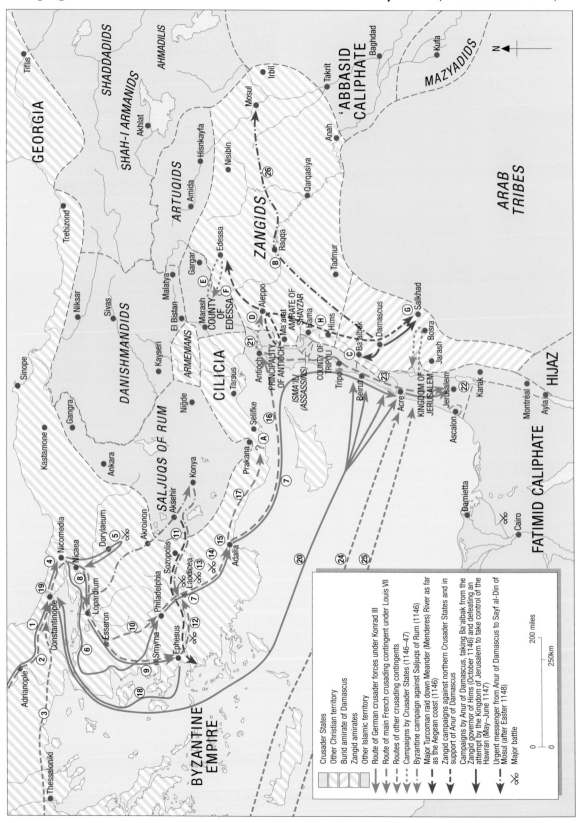

Crusader States
Other Christian territory
Burid amirate of Damascus
Zangid amirates
Other Islamic territory
Route of German crusader forces under Konrad III
Route of main French crusading contingent under Louis VII
Routes of other crusading contingents
Campaigns by Crusader States (1146–47)
Byzantine campaign against Saljuqs of Rum (1146)
Major Turcoman raid down Meander (Menderes) River as far as the Aegean coast (1146)
Zangid campaigns against northern Crusader States and in support of Anur of Damascus
Campaigns by Anur of Damascus, taking Ba'albak from the Zangid governor of Hims (October 1146) and defeating an attempt by the Kingdom of Jerusalem to take control of the Hawran (May–June 1147)
Urgent messenger from Anur of Damascus to Sayf al-Din of Mosul (after Easter 1148)
Major battle

0   200 miles
0   250km

Events prior to the arrival of the Second Crusade

A Thrust by Saljuqs of Rum temporarily takes Prakana, threatening to cut the Byzantine coastal road.

B Assassination of 'Imad al-Din during his siege of Qal'at Jabar (14 September 1146).

C Anur of Damascus takes Ba'albak from the Zangid governor of Hims (October 1146).

D Prince Raymond of Antioch raids almost as far as Aleppo (September 1146).

E Count Jocelin II temporarily retakes Edessa from Nur al-Din (October–November 1146).

F Nur al-Din counter-raids the territory of Antioch but withdraws to retake Edessa (November 1146).

G Altuntash, governor of the Hawran, rebels against Anur of Damascus, offers the province to King Baldwin III of Jerusalem who arrives to take control; they are defeated by Anur and Nur al-Din (May–June 1147).

H Nur al-Din brings his army to support Anur against Altuntash (May–June 1147), then returns to Aleppo after the defeat of Baldwin and Altuntash (July 1147).

The Second Crusade

1 Konrad III of Germany reaches Constantinople (10 September 1147).

2 Louis VII of France reaches Constantinople (4–5 October 1147).

3 Amadeus II of Savoy joins Louis in Constantinople.

4 Konrad III leads the German crusader army to Nicomedia then divides his forces, intending to take the strongest part across Saljuq central Anatolia while the baggage train, pilgrims and a defending force under Bishop Otto of Freising take a more westerly route.

5 Konrad III's force is forced to turn back, several days' march beyond Dorylaeum (25 October 1147), then retreats under Turkish harassment to Nicaea.

6 Bishop Otto's force follows the coastal road then turns inland, probably up the Gediz River via Philadelphia to Laodicea.

7 Bishop Otto's force is ambushed, probably just outside Laodicea; the survivors continue to Adalia (Antalya) from where they sail for the Holy Land.

8 Louis VII and Amadeus II march to Nicaea where they hear of Konrad's defeat; they send a military escort for the Germans and agree to rendezvous with Konrad at Lopardium.

9 The combined forces of Louis and Konrad march via Esseron (mid-November 1147), Pergamon and Smyrna to Ephesus where they celebrate Christmas; the crusader camp is attacked by Turkish raiders outside Ephesus.

10 Part of the French crusader army takes the direct route to Philadelphia, which they reach safely, probably then awaiting the main army at Laodicea.

11 A large Saljuq and Danishmandid army assembles west of Konya; Emperor Manuel warns the crusader leaders.

12 Louis VII, Amadeus II and the French crusader army leave Ephesus (28 December 1147), ascend the Meander Valley, defeat a Turkish ambush (1 January 1148) and reach Laodicea (3 January 1148) but are refused entry by the Byzantine governor.

13 The French crusader army is attacked while crossing the flank of Mount Cadmus (Honaz Dagi) via the Kazik Beli Pass, suffering major losses (c. 8 January 1148).

14 The French crusader army is again ambushed, probably while crossing the headwaters of the Dalaman River.

15 The French crusader army reaches Adalia but is refused entry (20 January 1148).

16 Lack of available shipping obliges Louis VII to divide his forces; the knights and best troops accompany him to Saint-Simeon (arriving 19 March 1148).

17 Large numbers of pilgrims, non-combatants and infantry are left at Adalia under Count Thierry of Flanders and Count Archambaud VII of Bourbon; they try to continue along the coastal road; it is not known how many succeed, though Count Thierry of Flanders certainly reaches Jerusalem.

18 Konrad III falls sick and returns to Constantinople by sea from Ephesus (January 1148); the majority of his troops probably return overland.

19 Many German pilgrims and troops abandon their crusade while Emperor Manuel provides cash and military supplies to re-equip what remains of Konrad III's army.

20 Konrad III and his re-equipped crusader army sail from Constantinople (7 March 1148) in a Byzantine fleet; the fleet is scattered by storms and arrives at several different ports.

21 Louis and the French crusader army remain in Antioch but there are rumours of an affair between his wife, Eleanor of Aquitaine, and Prince Raymond of Antioch.

22 Konrad III, Baldwin II, Patriarch Fulcher of Jerusalem and a senior representative of the Templars agree that Damascus rather than Edessa will be the primary target of the Second Crusade (Easter 1148).

23 Louis VII marches south (late May or early June 1148), then visits Christian shrines in Jerusalem (early June 1148).

24 Southern French crusaders under Count Alphonse-Jordan of Toulouse arrive by sea (April 1148) but Alphonse-Jordan dies suddenly at Caesarea, resulting in the accusation that he had been poisoned by Count Raymond II of Tripoli.

25 An unknown proportion of the northern European naval crusade arrives (April or May 1148).

26 Anur sends an urgent request for military assistance to Sayf al-Din of Mosul (probably a few days after the Easter meeting of Konrad, Baldwin, et al.)

lands and the Prince of Antioch wanted a campaign that would roll back recent Islamic advances, many in the Kingdom of Jerusalem now believed that the twice lost and twice sacked city of Edessa was no longer worth retaking. Some argued that the northern Syrian city of Aleppo was a more suitable target, or perhaps the formidable Arab-Islamic frontier fortress and independent state of Shayzar. Then there was Fatimid-held Ascalon, which many barons of the Kingdom of Jerusalem regarded as a strategic threat despite the declining power of the Fatimid Caliphate. As yet there seem to have been few voices arguing in favour of attacking Damascus.

Traditionally, almost all historians of the Crusades have maintained that the decision to attack Damascus was an act of inexplicable folly. More recently, a favourable interpretation has been placed upon what was undoubtedly a daring strategic decision. In fact it is possible that Damascus, like Ascalon, was already regarded as a 'natural' part of the Kingdom of Jerusalem that had yet to be conquered. It has even been suggested that anticipation of its eventual conquest meant that the rulers of Jerusalem would not allow the crusader Principality of Galilee to grow too strong, perhaps fearing that it might seize Damascus and thus become a rival to Jerusalem.

Most historians have also regarded the Second Crusade's decision to attack Damascus as flawed because of a traditional alliance between that city and the Kingdom of Jerusalem. In reality Damascus remained the crusaders' only real rival in southern Syria, and the rulers of Jerusalem naturally wanted to stop both Damascus and the disputed Hawran region becoming a base from which attacks could be launched in the future.

Attempts had been made against Damascus before, notably in 1126 and 1129, so if this new assault succeeded it might perhaps have placed the Crusader States in a better position to face the more formidable enemy who was already emerging in northern Syria – Nur al-Din of Aleppo. Above all there was a fear – amply justified by future events – that a weak Damascus would soon be taken over by Nur al-Din.

MUSLIM PLANS

A mid-12th century Benedictine document from the Abbey of St Petrus in Csatár may be one of the earliest surviving medieval Hungarian manuscripts. It is largely based upon Byzantine art and indicates the close cultural links between Hungary and the Byzantine Empire. (*Gebhard-Bibel*, Cod. ser. nov. 4236, Osterreichische Nationalbibliothek, Vienna)

Being on the receiving end of a massive invasion, the political and military leaders of the Islamic Middle East could initially do little more than wait and see what their enemies would do. The first to be attacked was Sultan Ma'sud of the Saljuq Sultanate of Rum in Anatolia, who would almost certainly have known of the threat since late 1146. This was probably why he offered peace to the Byzantine emperor, despite the latter's very recent invasion of the sultanate. Thereafter the strength of Saljuq Rumi forces enabled Sultan Mas'ud to take the tactical offensive, hitting the crusader armies while they were still inside nominally Byzantine territory.

Anur of Damascus had no such luxury. He had to rely upon traditional Islamic defensive warfare and counter-siege measures as described in several Islamic military manuals from this period and earlier.

The Zangid rulers Nur al-Din and Sayf al-Din may initially have felt as threatened as the Saljuq Sultan of Rum. However, they were in a strategically strong position that allowed them to watch and wait while assembling their forces. As ruler of Aleppo, Nur al-Din was more exposed than his brother so his first action was to strengthen frontier positions facing the crusaders in Antioch. Here Prince Raymond was left to face Nur al-Din alone, with very few troops once King Louis VII had moved south to Jerusalem with his army. The departure of the French crusader contingent also left the remnants of the County of Edessa exposed to the Saljuqs of Rum as well as to Nur al-Din.

Meanwhile, Anur of Damascus clearly did more than merely await events. One of the most important unanswered questions concerning the Second Crusade is just when Anur asked his Zangid neighbours for support. What is known is that Anur destroyed wells and watering places along the enemy's anticipated line of approach. Here he was helped by the fact that the crusaders had few options and their watering places were few in number. Their strategy proved to be similar to that of several previous invaders from the same direction, including 10th-century Fatimid Egyptian armies.

THE CAMPAIGN

Perhaps the most significant event in Syria after the retaking of Edessa by the Muslims was not a battle but a wedding, the marriage of Anur of Damascus' daughter Ismat al-Din to Nur al-Din, the new ruler of Aleppo, in 1147. Although this was a political alliance, cementing the growing links between the two states, Ismat al-Din was more than a mere pawn. She came from a Turkish family, a social class and a cultural group in which women had traditionally played a prominent political as well as cultural role. One of her most notable predecessors was Zumurrud Khatun Bint Jawli, sister of Malik Duqaq, wife of Buri Ibn Tughtakin, mother of his sons Isma'il and Mahmud and effectively co-ruler of Damascus in the early 1130s. As well as conducting successful campaigns against the crusaders, Zumurrud Khatun also fought against 'Imad al-Din Zangi of Mosul, before marrying him in 1138 and moving to Aleppo, where she largely retired from politics.

Mu'in al-Din Anur became *atabeg* of Damascus in the same year that Zumurrud moved to Aleppo. He himself soon married the widowed mother of the current *malik* or prince of Damascus, a woman whose status as Saljuq royal princess greatly strengthened Anur's prestige and power. These Seljuq women also played a significant role in cultural life; Zumurrud Khatun founded three mosques in and around Damascus while Anur's daughter, Ismat al-Din, established one of the city's new Sunni *madrasas* in 1146. Several of these buildings would be mentioned during the course of the siege of 1148. It is also interesting to note that at around the same time that Zumurrud was a political force in Damascus, Melisende was the similarly powerful Queen of Jerusalem.

Improving relations between Nur al-Din and Anur undermined Melisende's policy of maintaining an alliance with Damascus, and she may even have encouraged a rebellion by Altuntash, the Muslim Armenian governor of the Hawran in May 1147. He then offered to hand the fortresses of Busra and Salkhad over to the Franks in return for cash. An embassy from Jerusalem to Damascus optimistically suggested that the crusader kingdom should take over the Hawran and re-establish its alliance with Damascus. Anur wanted the alliance, but was certainly not prepared to abandon the Islamic towns and peoples of the Hawran, an area which was strategically and economically vital to Damascus. So he led his army to Salkhad while also calling for help from his son-in-law Nur al-Din. By the time King Baldwin III led his army to take possession of Busra and Salkhad, Anur and Nur al-Din had already joined forces. After some fighting the Franks retreated, but even at this point Anur stopped his victorious troops from pursuing the enemy too closely, not wanting to make relations with the crusader kingdom worse than they already were.

According to some sources Altuntash fled to Jerusalem, but Baldwin or Melisende, not wanting to break with Damascus entirely, expelled the ex-governor who, rather naively, returned to Damascus. There a legal tribunal ordered him to be blinded as punishment for having his own brother blinded, after which, as the chronicler Abu Shama wrote, 'he was allowed to remain at liberty and to live in a house he owned in Damascus' (Abu Shama, 1989; 52–53).

By June 1147, the first overland contingents of the Second Crusade were already on their way east, led by the German crusading army under Konrad III. However, Konrad's hope that it would remain a professional force of trained soldiers was in vain, and, according to Gerhoh of Reichersberg, the army was almost immediately joined by 'a multitude of peasants and servants, abandoning their ploughs and their services'. It followed the Danube River, moving in stages with some troops travelling by land while others were transported in ships. The presence of Boris, a claimant to the Hungarian throne who had recently tried to invade the country, might have caused problems, so the crusader leaders agreed to conceal him – or perhaps King Geza of Hungary chose to ignore the fact he was there. Nevertheless tensions between the Germans and Hungarians remained, despite Geza's policy of helping the crusaders in any way he could.

The French set off shortly after the Germans, Pope Eugenius and Bernard of Clairvaux having preached to a huge assembly at the Abbey of Saint-Denis outside Paris in June 1147 to mark King Louis's departure. After crossing the German imperial frontier, Louis's troops paused at Metz where they were joined by other contingents. They next paused at Worms, to be joined by Norman and Anglo-Norman contingents under Bishop Arnulf of Lisieux. Unfortunately a quarrel with local merchants broke out and around this time a substantial body of men, worried by the cost of food, broke away from the main army and travelled via Italy. A different problem surfaced at Ratisbon

LEFT
The old centre of the little town of Mizzah where the Second Crusade paused briefly before launching itself against the Syrian capital. (Author's photograph)

RIGHT
The southern wall of the Saljuq citadel of Damascus where the Banyas Canal flowed out of the citadel. (Author's photograph)

(Regensburg) with an ominous culture clash between King Louis's courtiers and an embassy sent by Emperor Manuel of Byzantium.

Nevertheless, good forward planning meant that both the French and the Germans got across Germany, Hungary and most of the Byzantine Balkans without significant problems. The Byzantine authorities provided the food supplies that had already been agreed upon while the Germans similarly stuck to their agreements. Nevertheless, camp-followers, who lacked carts or sufficient baggage animals, started to suffer hunger as they crossed Thrace, the final Byzantine province before reaching Constantinople. Meanwhile, a Byzantine military force either observed or escorted the Germans. It was commanded by Prosuch, an officer of Turkish origin who had led a Byzantine invasion of the crusader Principality of Antioch just over two years earlier. According to the Byzantine chronicler Kinnamos, the Germans burned down an Orthodox monastery near Adrianople (Edirne) in revenge for the reported murder of one of their sick men by local people and in Kinnamos' version of events Prosuch drove the German troublemakers away and inflicted casualties. Under such circumstances Manuel though it prudent to prepare the defences of his capital.

The French crusaders under Louis VII defeated a Saljuq ambush in the Meander Valley, well inside nominal Byzantine territory. (Author's photograph)

What happened next was seen by some as divine punishment for the Germans' lack of discipline. It certainly reflected a lack of local geographical and climate knowledge. On 7 September 1147 the German army was caught in a flash flood at Choirobakchoi, not far from Constantinople, which resulted in huge losses of equipment, money and supplies as well as some fatalities, mostly amongst the camp followers. They had, in fact, set up camp between two dry river beds at the upper end of an inlet from the Sea of Marmara known as the Arm of St George (today Büyükçekmece). This, on top of weariness and declining morale, resulted in many of the crusaders going home.

Three days later the bedraggled German crusaders reached the Byzantine imperial capital of Constantinople, where there was a frosty exchange of letters between Konrad and Manuel while the German crusaders made camp at Pera (Galata) on the northern side of the Golden Horn. Some of the crusaders now sacked the Philopation pleasure park but were also worsted in a clash with Prosuch and his small force of Turkish mercenaries because, in the opinion of the chronicler Kinnamos, the Byzantines were 'superior in military science and perseverance in battle'. The Emperor Manuel clearly did not want further difficulties with this first crusader army, especially as the French were only a few days behind and the Siculo-Normans from Italy were already causing difficulties in Greece. So he ordered that a full-scale effort should transport the Germans across the Bosphorus as quickly as possible.

As the French marched across the Balkans they used bridges and other crossing equipment that the Germans had left for them. However, they may also have found that local food supplies were exhausted, leaving them even more dependent upon the Byzantine authorities. In the event, French discipline proved superior to that of the Germans and there were few cases of pillaging. Nevertheless, relations again deteriorated as this second crusading army neared Constantinople. Some of its commanders even suggested attacking the Byzantine capital and a full-scale confrontation seems to have been avoided only through the Emperor Manuel's diplomatic skills.

Events away to the west in Greece and Albania certainly contributed to heightened tension; King Roger of Sicily's fleet was raiding the western coasts of the Byzantine Empire even as the French crusaders neared Constantinople.

Meanwhile Byzantine authority in those provinces of western Anatolia that the crusaders would soon cross varied from area to area. On the coasts it was reasonably effective but even here local governors remained highly suspicious of the crusaders. In the mountains Byzantine rule ranged from tentative to merely nominal with many areas being used as grazing by both Byzantine peasants and Turkish nomads. Nor had the Saljuq Turkish ruler of the Anatolians been idle. Sultan Ma'sud was clearly well informed, and as the crusader armies approached he asked for military help from his Muslim neighbours. The rumoured size of the crusader army was terrifying, and Ma'sud, like his troops, would have recalled the success of the First Crusade half a century earlier.

News of the forthcoming invasion also reached Syria, along with accounts of how the Saljuq Sultanate of Rum was readying itself to face the threat. In his *Kitab al-Rawdatayn*, Abu Shama quoted an earlier observer describing how 'local governors had prepared their defences, assembled troops who had gone to defend all the defiles which allowed access into Muslim territory, to stop them breaking through. At the same time mobile columns had been sent to harass the enemy's line of march and by vigorous attacks bring death and destruction to them' (Abu Shama, 1898; 54–55).

Rumours about German victories made the French keen to press ahead but the cautious and perhaps better informed King Louis insisted on waiting until his army was joined by other contingents, including an army led by Count Amadeus II of Savoy. Then came news of the Germans' startling

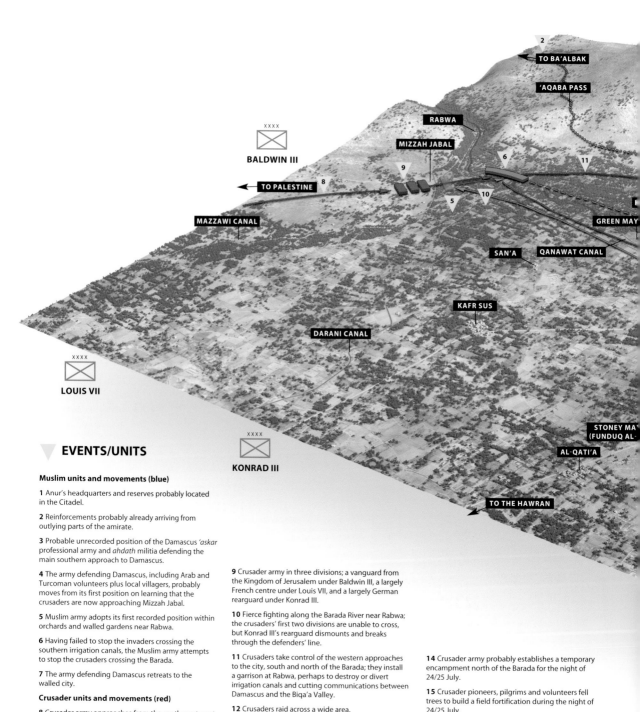

Map labels:
- TO BA'ALBAK
- 'AQABA PASS
- RABWA
- MIZZAH JABAL
- BALDWIN III (xxxx)
- TO PALESTINE
- MAZZAWI CANAL
- GREEN MAY...
- SAN'A
- QANAWAT CANAL
- KAFR SUS
- DARANI CANAL
- LOUIS VII (xxxx)
- STONEY MA... (FUNDUQ AL-...)
- AL-QATI'A
- KONRAD III (xxxx)
- TO THE HAWRAN

EVENTS/UNITS

Muslim units and movements (blue)

1 Anur's headquarters and reserves probably located in the Citadel.

2 Reinforcements probably already arriving from outlying parts of the amirate.

3 Probable unrecorded position of the Damascus *'askar* professional army and *ahdath* militia defending the main southern approach to Damascus.

4 The army defending Damascus, including Arab and Turcoman volunteers plus local villagers, probably moves from its first position on learning that the crusaders are now approaching Mizzah Jabal.

5 Muslim army adopts its first recorded position within orchards and walled gardens near Rabwa.

6 Having failed to stop the invaders crossing the southern irrigation canals, the Muslim army attempts to stop the crusaders crossing the Barada.

7 The army defending Damascus retreats to the walled city.

Crusader units and movements (red)

8 Crusader army approaches from the south-west, past or through Mizzah Jabal, having formed up in battle array near Darayya.

9 Crusader army in three divisions; a vanguard from the Kingdom of Jerusalem under Baldwin III, a largely French centre under Louis VII, and a largely German rearguard under Konrad III.

10 Fierce fighting along the Barada River near Rabwa; the crusaders' first two divisions are unable to cross, but Konrad III's rearguard dismounts and breaks through the defenders' line.

11 Crusaders take control of the western approaches to the city, south and north of the Barada; they install a garrison at Rabwa, perhaps to destroy or divert irrigation canals and cutting communications between Damascus and the Biqa'a Valley.

12 Crusaders raid across a wide area.

13 Crusader raiders destroy the suburb of Faradis on 24 or early 25 July.

14 Crusader army probably establishes a temporary encampment north of the Barada for the night of 24/25 July.

15 Crusader pioneers, pilgrims and volunteers fell trees to build a field fortification during the night of 24/25 July.

16 Crusader army's main siege position outside the Bab al-Jabiya.

THE FIRST CRUSADER ASSAULT ON DAMASCUS
24 July until the morning of 25 July 1148

A note on scale: the base map shows an area 7km wide x 6.25km deep

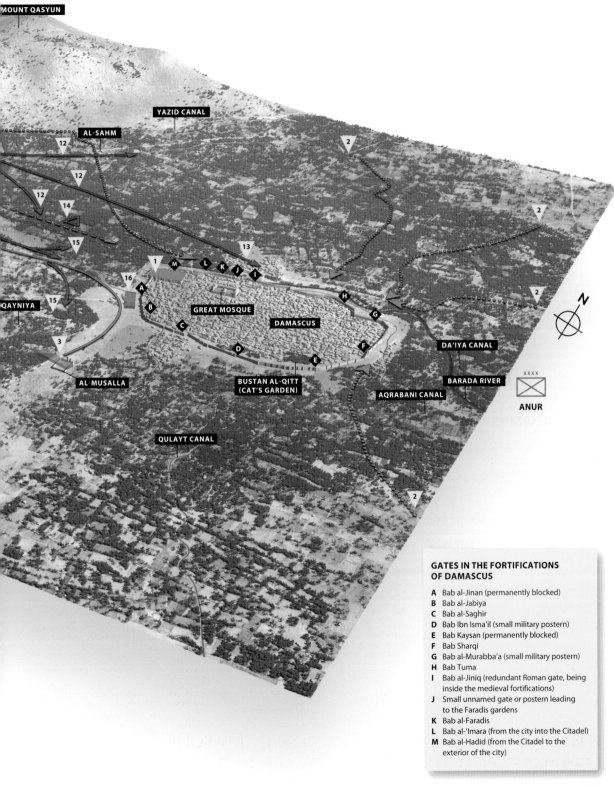

MOUNT QASYUN

YAZID CANAL

AL-SAHM

12

12

12

14

15

QAYNIYA

15

3

1

16

A

B

C

D

E

M L K J I

13

GREAT MOSQUE

DAMASCUS

2

2

2

H

G

F

AL-MUSALLA

BUSTAN AL-QITT
(CAT'S GARDEN)

QULAYT CANAL

AQRABANI CANAL

DA'IYA CANAL

BARADA RIVER

xxxx

ANUR

2

N

**GATES IN THE FORTIFICATIONS
OF DAMASCUS**

A Bab al-Jinan (permanently blocked)
B Bab al-Jabiya
C Bab al-Saghir
D Bab Ibn Isma'il (small military postern)
E Bab Kaysan (permanently blocked)
F Bab Sharqi
G Bab al-Murabba'a (small military postern)
H Bab Tuma
I Bab al-Jiniq (redundant Roman gate, being
     inside the medieval fortifications)
J Small unnamed gate or postern leading
     to the Faradis gardens
K Bab al-Faradis
L Bab al-'Imara (from the city into the Citadel)
M Bab al-Hadid (from the Citadel to the
     exterior of the city)

45

defeat. Rumours spread that the Byzantines intentionally kept the two crusading armies apart, and for a moment it seems that Louis might pull back to Adrianople (Edirne), to join King Roger of Sicily in an assault upon Constantinople. Nothing came of the idea but, with tensions rising, everyone was eager to get the French crusading army across the Bosphorus.

The circumstances of the German crusading army's defeat in its first attempt to cross Anatolia remain unclear. Perhaps Konrad was hoping to reach the Mediterranean before winter. He was still following in the footsteps of the First Crusade, which had taken longer to cross Anatolia than Konrad allowed himself. On the other hand, much of the Second Crusade's route would be through territory that the Byzantine Empire had supposedly reconquered, so perhaps Konrad anticipated a largely trouble-free march by properly equipped professional soldiers, while the baggage and poorly provisioned camp-followers took the slower coastal route, accompanied by a small detachment of troops under Otto of Freising. Unfortunately many of these people feared being abandoned and refused to be separated from the main body.

Quite what happened to Bishop Otto of Freising's command is even more obscure. He seems to have followed the Aegean coast before turning inland, probably up the Gediz River valley to Philadelphia (Alasehir). He then ran short of supplies, slaughtered many pack animals as food and then fell into a Turkish ambush, probably near Laodicea, losing many men killed or taken prisoner. Otto of Freising and the Bishop of Naumberg struggled on to the coast where most took ship for Syria, while others perhaps attempted to continue along the southern coast of Anatolia.

Meanwhile Konrad set out in late autumn when the high country was cold and lacked pasture. The medieval and modern roads from Nicea (Iznik) to Dorylaeum (Eskisehir) initially follow the fertile river valleys, making the

supply situation easier. Though Dorylaeum was still in ruins it remained an important communications junction surrounded by pastures that had earlier been used by an imperial stud. Abundant water and fodder were also why Turkoman pastoral tribes were attracted to the area, and the plain of Dorylaeum might have been home to the largest concentration of Turkoman nomads in western Anatolia during the 12th century (Roche, 2006; 85–98).

Though not a desert in the normal sense of the word, the region beyond Dorylaeum was infertile and largely uninhabited, and Konrad's troops began to run out of supplies after eight or ten days. Foraging was essential, but it took time and those involved were vulnerable to attack even while the crusaders were still inside nominally Byzantine territory. The main clash occurred on 25 October, though in fact there seems to have been a number of ambushes, one of which resulted in the death of Bernard of Plötzkau, a Saxon nobleman who was escorting stragglers and was the most senior man to be killed during Konrad's disastrous attempt to cross Anatolia.

With the situation getting worse and with the army perhaps three days' march beyond Dorylaeum, the German barons convinced Konrad that the army must turn back. So began a painful retreat to Dorylaeum and from there to Nicea, a partial eclipse of the sun on 26 October being seen by many as a sign of God's anger. Harassed virtually all the way by the Turks, the crusaders' retreat became a rout. Konrad was himself wounded by arrows and many of the weakest people simply fell behind to be captured. What remained of the German crusading army was now much reduced and, although its professional core remained largely intact, morale had been shaken. Not surprisingly, the reverse was true amongst the Turks and other Muslims, the anonymous Syriac Chronicle recording that 'The Turks grew rich for they had taken gold and silver like pebbles with no end' (Tritton and Gibb, 1933; 298).

Having crossed the Bosphorus, the French now supplied the battered Germans with money and supplies while the latter agreed to rendezvous with the French and Savoyards at Lopadion (Ulubat, near Karacabey) from where the combined crusader armies continued their march together.

ABOVE
Banyas, where the Second Crusade briefly paused on its march to Damascus. (Author's photograph)

BELOW
The Second Crusade climbed the Golan Heights then marched along the foothills of Mount Hermon, here seen behind what had been an Israeli strongpoint, subsequently used by the UN Observer Force north-east of Qunaytra. (Author's photograph)

Muslim units and movements (blue)

1 Anur's headquarters and reserves are located in the Citadel.

2 Prayers are held in the Great Mosque.

3 Volunteers arrive from outlying provinces.

4 Anur assembles the *'askar*, the *ahdath* and volunteers in or near the Citadel; they include Yusuf al-Finadalawi, whom Anur tries to dissuade from taking part (25 July).

5 The forces of Damascus launch a counter-attack through the northern gates to clear enemy forces from north of the Barada River (25 July) – almost certainly timed to coincide with the arrival of a substantial Lebanese force through the Barada gorge.

6 A major battle takes place in the area between Lower Nayrab and Rabwa; the Muslims suffer significant casualties, including Nur al-Dawla (Saladin's elder brother), Yusuf al-Findalawi the legal scholar, and 'Abd al-Rahman al-Halhuli, but force the crusaders back across the river.

7 A force largely consisting of infantry archers arrives from the Biqa'a Valley, perhaps tipping the battle in favour of the Muslims.

8 The defenders also attempt to disrupt the completion of the crusaders' siege position outside Bab al-Jabiya.

9 The inhabitants of Damascus strengthen their defences using large baulks of timber (25–26 July).

10 On 26 and 27 July an increasing number of reinforcements reaches Damascus, mostly entering through Bab Tuma and Bab Sharqi.

11 Bands of Turcoman volunteers sent by Sayf al-Din arrive in Damascus from 26 July onwards; Anur may have received messages from Sayf al-Din and Nur al-Din on 26 July, and certainly by the 27th.

12 A guerrilla campaign against isolated groups of besiegers and their communications seems to begin on 26 July.

13 The defenders launch major assaults against the crusaders' siege positions on 26 and 27 July.

14 Sayf al-Din probably sends a message to the crusader leadership, warning them to break off the siege (26 or 27 July).

15 People of Damascus take over the abandoned crusader siege position on the morning of 29 July.

16 The retreating crusaders are harried by Turcoman troops.

Crusader units and movements (red)

17 Crusader leadership establishes its base camp on the Green Maydan (25 July).

18 Crusaders' main fortified siege position outside the Bab al-Jabiya gate.

19 A crusader unit occupies the Rabwa area until the end of the siege.

20 Crusader lines of communication are increasingly vulnerable to guerrilla attacks from 26 to 28 July.

21 According to a Muslim reference, the displaying of the Relic of the True Cross takes place on 26 or 27 July, to raise crusader morale. Elements within the crusader leadership are in communication with Anur from at least 27 July onwards.

22 On 26 or 27 July the crusader leadership decides to move its base camp; now that the defenders have regained the area north of the Barada River, it is vulnerable.

23 The Bishop of Langres makes a reconnaissance of the area south of Damascus, late on the 27th or early on 28 July; the areas of al-Battatin and al-Hayr were traditionally regarded as vulnerable parts of the city's defences. He reports that the area south of Damascus lacks food supplies, yet the crusader leadership plans to establish a new siege position there.

24 On 28 July, the crusaders begin to move their base camp from the Green Maydan, but only get as far as Qayniya, where they pause for the night of 28/29 July.

25 The crusaders abandon the siege of Damascus and retreat south, 29 July.

26 The crusader unit at Rabwa joins the retreat.

TO BA'ALBAK

'AQABA PASS

RABWA

MIZZAH JABAL

TO PALESTINE

MAZZAWI CANAL

GREEN MA

SAN'A

QANAWAT CANAL

KAFR SUS

DARANI CANAL

STONEY MA
(FUNDUQ AL-

AL-QATI'A

TO THE HAWRAN

XXXX
BALDWIN III

XXXX
LOUIS VII

XXXX
KONRAD III

THE BREAKING OF THE SIEGE
25–29 July 1148

A note on scale: the base map shows an area 7km wide x 6.25km deep

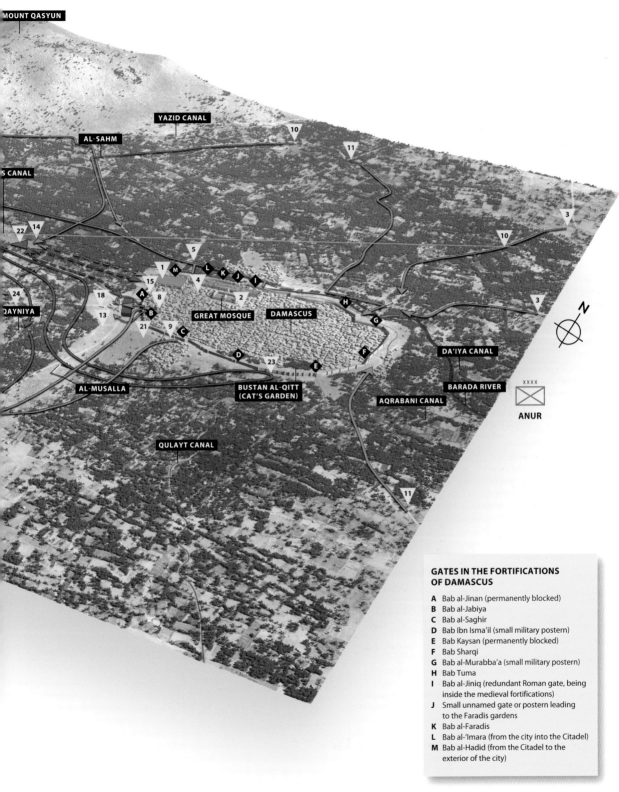

MOUNT QASYUN

YAZID CANAL

AL-SAHM

S CANAL

10

11

22 14

3

24

QAYNIYA

5

10

3

1 M L K J I

15 4

18 8 2

A

13 B

21 9 C GREAT MOSQUE DAMASCUS H

G

F

D

23 E

AL-MUSALLA

BUSTAN AL-QITT
(CAT'S GARDEN)

DA'IYA CANAL

BARADA RIVER xxxx

AQRABANI CANAL

ANUR

QULAYT CANAL

11

**GATES IN THE FORTIFICATIONS
OF DAMASCUS**

A Bab al-Jinan (permanently blocked)
B Bab al-Jabiya
C Bab al-Saghir
D Bab Ibn Isma'il (small military postern)
E Bab Kaysan (permanently blocked)
F Bab Sharqi
G Bab al-Murabba'a (small military postern)
H Bab Tuma
I Bab al-Jiniq (redundant Roman gate, being
      inside the medieval fortifications)
J Small unnamed gate or postern leading
      to the Faradis gardens
K Bab al-Faradis
L Bab al-'Imara (from the city into the Citadel)
M Bab al-Hadid (from the Citadel to the
      exterior of the city)

49

Their original destination had been Philadelphia (Alaşehir) and then Laodicea. Two roads were available and recent experience led Konrad to argue in favour of the coast. Louis agreed and most of the army followed this road though a few men stuck to the old plan, probably awaiting the main army at Laodicea where their successful 'short cut' perhaps undermined the arguments of those urging caution. In mid-November 1147 the main crusader force reached Esseron, but progress over the next four weeks was slow with many rivers to ford, and mountains and deep valleys to cross. Supply problems forced the troops to loot; many pack animals also died, while the inhabitants sought shelter for themselves and their animals within local fortifications.

After passing Pergamon (Bergama) and Smyrna (Izmir) the crusaders reached Ephesus (Efes) where they spent Christmas. Messages from Emperor Manuel warned that a large Turkish army was massing and that crusader behaviour was likely to cause some of the local inhabitants to seek revenge. By now the German army contained so many sick and wounded that it could not carry on without a period of rest, while Konrad was himself still suffering greatly from his wounds. In contrast, Louis wanted to press ahead, so in January 1148 Konrad sailed back to Constantinople to be placed under the care of Emperor Manuel's own physicians.

After Christmas, rain and snow fell for several days. Fearing that his army might be trapped by floods, Louis set out up the Meander Valley on 28 December. Although they were still deep inside the Byzantine frontier, the French crusaders were shadowed by a substantial Turkish force as they pressed inland. Louis carefully arranged his line of march with well-armed knights in the front, rear and flanks while the vulnerable baggage train and the wounded remained in the centre. As the French looked for a camping place on 1 January 1148, one Turkish unit attacked them from the rear while another attacked their vanguard at a ford across the Meander. This time, however, the attackers' withdrawal was too slow and they were hit by a counter charge, driving the enemy back with substantial losses.

Reaching Laodicia on 3 January, the French were by now in an area where Byzantine control was extremely tenuous and some even believed that the local Byzantine governor was in league with the enemy. In reality the

The local militias that defended Damascus made a stand along the Barada River and irrigation canals west of the city, south of what is now the Tishrin Public Park. (Author's photograph)

crusaders' necessary plundering for food led some of the Greek inhabitants to attack stragglers and occasionally to join forces with the Turks. The precise route taken by the crusaders from Laodicea to Adalia is unknown, though they clearly did not follow the ancient main road that ran through a no man's land between Byzantine and Saljuq territory. Instead, Louis led his army by minor roads across the massif then known as Mount Cadmus (Honaz Dagi), passing the spot where the German contingent led by Bishop Otto of Freising had been so disastrously ambushed.

The French army marched with most of the cavalry at the front, the baggage in the centre, and King Louis in command of the rearguard. The leadership of individual units was rotated daily to ensure that noblemen shared the honours. So it was that Geoffrey of Rancon and Count Amadeus II were jointly in charge of the vanguard when the crusader army faced its biggest logistical challenge – the crossing of Mount Cadmus on or around 8 January 1148.

The Kazik Beli Pass reaches a height of 1,250m and would take a full day to cross, the crusader army being very extended. However, the vanguard found their crossing easy and, being unopposed, ignored orders to pause. Instead they started down the other side of the pass, presumably to find a good place to camp. Now the French crusaders' excellent discipline and communications failed, the rest of the army not being informed of the vanguard's change of plan. Meanwhile the rearguard was held back to defend the foot of the pass, perhaps intending to cross next day. This left the cumbersome baggage train almost unprotected as it made its crossing.

The Turks seized this opportunity to attack, some taking control of the crest of the pass while others struck the baggage column, which may itself have been up to 10km long. Odo of Deuil was in the centre and observed the growing panic before he galloped back to King Louis, who may have been too far back to see what was happening. Louis rushed into action but the steep terrain made crusader cavalry charge tactics virtually impossible. Many of Louis's elite royal guard were killed and the king himself was almost captured, but their efforts enabled the baggage train to reach the crest. The vanguard also returned to help.

TOP, LEFT
After emerging from a gorge that separates Mount Hermon from the Anti-Lebanon range, the Barada River continued to flow through a shallow but relatively steep-sided valley towards the north-western corner of the old city of Damascus. (Antoinette Nicolle photograph)

TOP, RIGHT
This Syrian lectionary is one of the very few illustrated Syrian manuscripts from the 12th century. The bulk of the townsmen and volunteers who defended Damascus in 1148 would have looked much like this unarmoured warrior at the 'Execution of John the Baptist'. (*Syriac Lectionary*, Ms. Add. 7169, f. 9v, British Library, London)

Stragglers came in throughout the night, but the crusaders' losses had
been high and Turkish morale had been raised. King Louis now sought
tactical advice from those true 'Crusading professionals', the Templars. Odo
described what happened:

> Because the Turks were quick to flee, our men were commanded to endure,
> until they received an order, the attacks of the enemies, and to withdraw
> forthwith when recalled, even though they should be making a stand as
> originally commanded.

The new arrangements enabled the Crusaders to defeat a second attempt
to stop them. However, the Turks and Greeks had agreed upon a form of
scorched-earth policy which hurt the invaders without causing too much
damage to the local population, driving their flocks a day or so's march ahead
of the crusader column, grazing the land bare and denying the invaders
fodder for their animals. By the time the French crusaders reached Adalia

(Antalya) on 20 January, they were in bad shape. By then dramatic events had taken place far to the west, in the Iberian Peninsula: the Second Crusade's naval expedition had taken part in the Portuguese conquest of Lisbon. The future capital of Portugal actually fell on 24 October 1147, in what has been described as the only real success of the Second Crusade.

Despite the crusaders' beliefs to the contrary, the Byzantine fleet was in no position to collect Louis's battered army from Adalia and ship it to the Holy Land. Not enough vessels were available and the new year's sailing season had yet to start. Perhaps the crusaders also hoped or assumed that the northern fleet, which was currently stalled in southern Portugal, would have appeared in the eastern Mediterranean, just as its predecessors did during the First Crusade.

Despite recent losses, the French crusader army still had part of its baggage train, and King Louis initially wanted to keep his forces together by continuing his march along the coast. But this led to divisions amongst his senior men once they learned that there would be enough ships to take the elite of the army directly to Antioch. Eventually King Louis agreed to leave the bulk of the infantry and non-combatants to go overland while he and the best-equipped troops went by sea. After a three-day voyage they reached Saint-Simeon (Samanda in Turkish, Suwaydiya in Arabic), the port of Antioch, on 19 March 1148.

Louis left two senior men in command at Adalia, Count Thierry of Flanders and Count Archambaud VII of Bourbon, but it is not known how many of the rest of the army reached Antioch overland. Odo of Deuil bitterly reported that the Turks were more compassionate to the French survivors than were the Greeks, 3,000 'young men' going with the Turks without even being obliged to change their religion. Thierry of Flanders subsequently played a controversial role during the siege of Damascus whereas Archambaud VII earned renown by 'conducting the retreat' of the wreckage of the disastrous Second Crusade.

Konrad III set sail from Constantinople in mid-March 1148, Byzantine and crusader sources recording that the Byzantine Emperor Manuel supplied his army with money and military equipment as well as transport to the Holy

ABOVE
A peasant and a Cistercian monk lopping branches in a 12th-century, French Cistercian manuscript. Such tools would have been used by the Second Crusade as it battled through the dense vegetation that the defenders of Damascus hoped would slow the crusader assault. (Ms.173 f. 41, Bibliothèque Municipale, Dijon; E. Juvin photograph)

LEFT
Almost all accounts of the Second Crusade's siege of Damascus mention tall buildings in the surrounding irrigated Ghuta regions, from which local militias launched guerrilla attacks upon the besiegers. (Ex-J.H. Vincent & J.W. Lee, *Earthly Steps of the Man of Galilee*, New York 1894)

Land. However, things did not go smoothly and some ships were wrecked while others were scattered, arriving at different ports during the month of April. Nevertheless the Byzantine emperor's generosity meant that Konrad was able to recruit and equip a new army from pilgrims and others in the Holy Land.

Meanwhile, in Antioch, Count Raymond urged King Louis to use the crusade for its original purpose, if not regaining Edessa then at least strengthening the Crusader States in northern Syria. It was, of course, during this period that rumours began to circulate about an affair between Count Raymond and his niece Eleanor of Aquitaine, Louis's wife. In reality Raymond was probably trying to use his family relationship with Eleanor to press his case for a northern campaign. Even before Louis brought his army south, an important meeting was held in Jerusalem at Easter 1148. Here Konrad, King Baldwin III, Patriarch Fulcher and an unnamed representative of the Knights Templar decided that the Second Crusade should attack Damascus. Queen Melisende, as a traditional proponent of the alliance with Damascus, was apparently not part of this decision. The *atabeg* Anur almost certainly learned of this Easter decision and would have had much more time to seek help from the Zangid rulers of Mosul and Aleppo than is normally realized. Louis's determination to complete his pilgrimage prevented Konrad from doing anything further until the French king was ready, and as a result the spring campaigning season was lost. Quite how many of the men who had helped capture Lisbon continued their voyage to the Middle East is unknown, though some Germans certainly did so.

On 24 June 1148 the senior leaders of the Second Crusade joined the ruler and barons of Jerusalem in a great conference near Acre. The Count of Tripoli sent no representative, having been blamed, almost certainly unjustly, for the death of Count Alphonse-Jordan of Toulouse. The latter led a Provençal crusader contingent that arrived by sea, but Alphonse-Jordan then died suddenly. His son, Bertrand of Toulouse, accused his cousin, Raymond of Tripoli, of poisoning the count, and as a result many Provençals went straight back home. The debate at Palmarea was long, and, although various ideas were proposed, the most powerful noblemen of Jerusalem urged an attack upon Damascus. They included men like Guy of Beirut, who stood to gain a great deal from the conquest of Damascus. Furthermore, it was in

Members of the old Arab aristocracy of the Middle East still played a major military role in the 12th century, though this was more characteristic of the Fatimid Caliphate of Egypt than of Syria. (Inv. I. 13, Keir Collection, London)

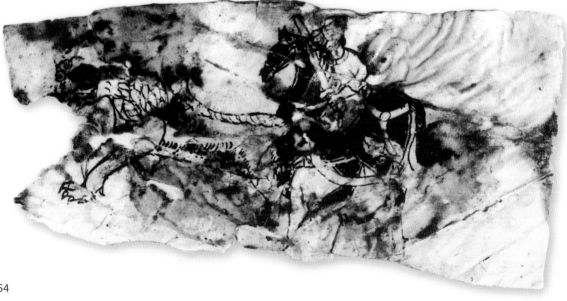

King Baldwin's interests to have Damascus and perhaps also the Hawran region in the hands of a loyal supporter like Guy.

Meanwhile, Mu'in al-Din Anur prepared himself for war, summoning help from Arab tribes and the governors of frontier provinces while posting scouting units on the roads leading to Damascus. Equally importantly, he sent men to cut off or divert sources of water in those areas that the invaders would have to cross. It has been widely suggested that the Zanfid rulers of Mosul and Aleppo could not have brought troops close enough to Damascus in time to have a real impact upon the campaign. However, given the nature of Islamic military organization and the time of year, it would probably have been possible for both to set out with their elite *'askar* troops within days of receiving the request. Anur's first appeal seems to have been sent to Sayf al-Din Ghazi in Mosul, as the senior Zangid ruler, and if this was done after the Easter meeting between Baldwin and Konrad there is no reason why Zangid forces could not have reached Hims, as claimed by several Arab chroniclers.

Once the army of the Kingdom of Jerusalem assembled, it joined the crusader contingents near Tiberius with the greatest religious relic in Christendom, a supposed fragment of the True Cross. Contemporary estimates of the size of medieval armies are notoriously unreliable but the crusader force was said to number 50,000 men. Whatever the true number, this was a formidable army, which, being accompanied by baggage animals, camels and cattle to be slaughtered as food, needed substantial supplies of food and water.

After consulting with local frontier experts in Baniyas, the crusaders took a road that ran across the southern slopes of Mount Hermon before descending through the Wadi al-'Ajam and crossing the A'waj River. At Manazil al-'Asakir (or 'The Dismounting Place of Soldiers') the invaders found that Anur's men had broken or diverted the water supply. So, the crusaders probably pulled back and made camp near Kiswa for the night of 23 July.

The densely packed houses and workshops of medieval Damascus were vulnerable to fire. Traditionally the upper parts of ordinary buildings were built of wood and mud brick, while the lower parts were of stone. (Author's photograph)

The march to Damascus, May to 23 July 1148

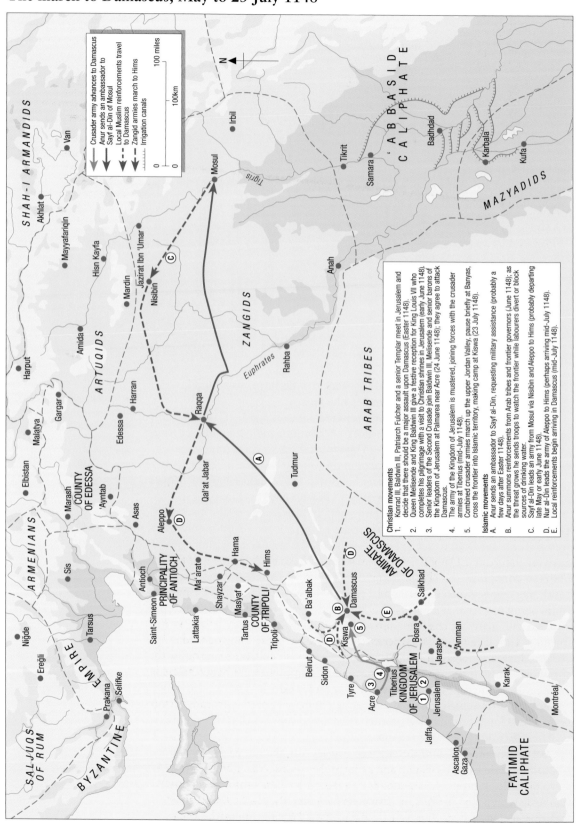

Legend:
- Crusader army advances to Damascus
- Anur sends an ambassador to Sayf al-Din of Mosul
- Local Muslim reinforcements travel to Damascus
- Zangid armies march to Hims
- Irrigation canals

100 miles
100km

Christian movements

1. Konrad III, Baldwin III, Patriarch Fulcher and a senior Templar meet in Jerusalem and decide that there should be a major assault upon Damascus (Easter 1148).

2. Queen Melisende and King Baldwin III give a festive reception for King Louis VII who completes his pilgrimage with a visit to Christian shrines in Jerusalem (early June 1148).

3. Senior leaders of the Second Crusade join Baldwin III, Melisende and senior barons of the Kingdom of Jerusalem at Palmarea near Acre (24 June 1148); they agree to attack Damascus.

4. The army of the Kingdom of Jerusalem is mustered, joining forces with the crusader armies at Tiberius (mid-July 1148).

5. Combined crusader armies march up the upper Jordan Valley, pause briefly at Banyas, cross the frontier into Islamic territory, making camp at Kiswa (23 July 1148).

Islamic movements

A. Anur sends an ambassador to Sayf al-Din, requesting military assistance (probably a few days after Easter 1148).

B. Anur summons reinforcements from Arab tribes and frontier governors (June 1148); as the threat grows he sends troops to watch the frontier while labourers divert or block sources of drinking water.

C. Sayf al-Din leads an army from Mosul via Nisibin and Aleppo to Hims (probably departing late May or early June 1148).

D. Nur al-Din leads the army of Aleppo to Hims (perhaps arriving mid-July 1148).

E. Local reinforcements begin arriving in Damascus (mid-July 1148).

DAMASCUS IS REACHED

Early on Saturday 24 July the crusader army crossed low hills north of Kiswa, perhaps changing an original intention to approach Damascus from the south, and moved into the Shahura Valley where they reached the outskirts of the irrigated area. They probably halted between the villages of Darayya and Mizzah from where the minarets of Damascus could be seen. The invaders would not have tried to establish themselves within orchards west of the Mazzawi irrigation canal. In fact, the dense cultivation around the city would soon prove a major obstacle. The crusaders were nevertheless in an area where they were guaranteed water and food.

William of Tyre provides a detailed account of how the crusader army now arrayed itself for battle:

> At Daria [Darayya], since the city was now so near, the sovereigns drew up their forces in battle formation and assigned the legions to their proper places in the order of march ... Because of its supposed familiarity with the country, the division led by the King of Jerusalem [Baldwin III] was, by the common decision of the princes, directed to lead the way and open a path for the legions

The fiercest fighting during the Second Crusade's assault upon the city of Damascus was outside the Jabiya Gate (left – from the outside; right – from the inside) at the western end of what Europeans know as 'The Street Called Straight'. In the mid-12th century the Bab al-Jabiya still consisted of a triple-arched Roman entrance, though two of these arches had been walled up. (Author's photographs)

following. To the King of the Franks [Louis VII] and his army was assigned the second place or centre, that they might aid those ahead if need arose. By the same authority, the Emperor [Konrad III] was to hold the third or rear position, in readiness to resist the enemy if, perchance, an attack should be made from behind. (Babcock and Krey, 1976; 187)

The fighting between the crusaders and the defenders of Damascus on Saturday 24 July went in favour of the attackers and focused upon a small area where the Barada River and its irrigation canals emerged from a narrow valley. Muslim Christian accounts of how the defenders resisted on 24 July are sketchy, though the professional army, Turkoman mercenaries, Syrian villagers and *ahdath* militia combined in an effort to stop the crusaders reaching the river and irrigation canals, two of which brought water directly into Damascus itself. There was bitter fighting in the orchards and narrow, walled lanes, but it was not until the crusaders reached the Barada River that they were halted, at least for a while.

Having failed to stop the enemy reaching the Barada, the Muslims now attempted to stop them crossing it, then cutting the road to Lebanon and sweeping round to attack Damascus from the north. According to William of Tyre:

The cavalry forces of the townsmen and of those who had come to their assistance realized that our army was coming through the orchards in order to besiege the city and they accordingly approached the stream which flowed by the town. This they did with their bows and their ballistas [crossbows] so that they could fight off the Latin army. (Brundage, 1976; 115–21)

Unfortunately William of Tyre's dramatic account fails to explain how the crusader rearguard made its way through those in front without the entire array collapsing into confusion:

The emperor [Konrad], in command of the forces following, demanded to know why the army did not advance. He was told that the enemy was in possession of the river and would not allow our forces to pass. Enraged at this news, Konrad and his knights galloped swiftly forward through the king's lines and reached the fighters who were trying to win the river. Here all leaped down from their horses and became foot soldiers, as is the custom of the Teutons when a desperate crisis occurs'. (Babcock and Krey, 1976; 189)

Abu Shama's account of the crusaders' success explains how the crusader army came to control both sides of the Barada:

Despite the multitude of *ahdath* [militia], Turks, warriors, and the common people of the town, volunteers and soldiers who had come from the provinces and had joined with them, the Muslims were overwhelmed by the enemy's numbers and were defeated by the infidels. The latter crossed the river, found themselves in the gardens and made camp there … The Franks…cut down trees to make palisades. They destroyed the orchards and passed the night in these tasks. (Abu Shama, 1898; 58–59)

It seems as though the invaders also immediately began constructing a fortified siege position south of the river, facing Bab al-Jabiya where Damascus was not protected by the Barada, while a large part of the army also spent that first night of the siege north of the Barada, where they not only had the river between themselves and the defending garrison but were

'Guard outside the Holy Sepulchre' in a 12th-century Syriac manuscript. He is armed with a spear whose blade is almost long enough to be called a pole-arm. (*Syriac Lectionary*, Ms. Add. 7169, f. 9v, British Library, London)

KING LOUIS VII TAKES REFUGE ON A ROCK DURING THE BATTLE OF MOUNT CADMUS (8 JANUARY 1148) (pp. 60–61)

The centre of the French crusader column containing the army's baggage train, was attacked by a large Turkish force as it crossed the Kazik Beli Pass just south of Mount Cadmus (Honaz Daği) in south-western Turkey. The Turks seem to have been joined by Byzantine Greek bandits and members of the local peasantry whose homes, crops and flocks had been looted by the hungry crusaders. King Louis VII and his personal retinue of knights and sergeants hurried up from the rearguard to protect the baggage, but soon got into trouble. Louis himself was either thrown from his horse or the animal was shot down by the enemies' arrows. So the king grasped a tree and hauled himself onto a rock where he was able to fend off his foes until help

arrived. The French eventually got across the pass, but not before they suffered significant losses, particularly amongst their senior men.

Louis is shown here on top of the rock (**1**), looking down towards a substantial number of Turks (**2**) plus members of the local peasantry (**3**) who are trying to attack him. Louis is using his large shield (**4**) to protect himself from the arrows. The king's injured horse lies dying nearby (**5**). Coming to Louis' aid are other French crusaders (**6**). Meanwhile, some of the Byzantine Greek bandits (**7**) and Muslim heavy cavalry (**8**) are clearly more keen on capturing the baggage or booty rather than getting at King Louis.

able to stop reinforcements reaching Damascus from Lebanon. The following day they established a more permanent camp south of the river but west of their fortified siege position.

On Sunday 25 July 1148 the crusaders began their attack, and the king established his camp on the Maydan al-Akhdar (Green Maydan) – the 'grassy cavalry training ground' watered by the Banyas canal, and an ideal spot for the crusaders to pasture their war horses. Abu Shama states: 'They came close to the city and established themselves on a position which in every period, ancient or recent, no besieging army had taken', perhaps referring to the crusaders' brief occupation of the cultivated zone between the city and Mount Qasyun. Ibn 'Asakir's subsequent statement that the Faradis suburb was 'now in ruins' as a result of the Second Crusade shows how far the invaders reached on the northern side of Damascus.

ANUR TRIES TO PURSUADE AL-FINDALAWI NOT TO GO WITH THE AHDATH MILITIA TO FIGHT THE INVADING CRUSADERS (25 JULY 1148) (pp. 64–65)

In this scene, the *ahdath* militia of Damascus has assembled inside the city of Damascus, near one of the northern gates, ready to join the government's *'askar* or small professional army in a major counter-attack against crusader forces that are raiding across a large area north of the Barada River.

The *ahdath* was a properly organized force, consisting of units led by officers and identified by its own flags. Largely recruited from younger men of the artisan and merchant classes, it also involved more senior members of society.

The street is very crowded, with highly excited people trying to get to their units or leaders that are identified by coloured flags. Anur (**1**), the atabeg or in effect the governor and military commander of Damascus, is accompanied by his Turkish guards (**2** and **3**). They are the only men to be mounted, with all the militia being on foot. Amongst the latter are men of all ages.

On this desperate occasion the militia has been joined by volunteers, including the aging legal scholar Yusuf al-Findalawi (**4**), who stands out with his long white beard. Al-Finadalawi is accompanied by the ascetic al-Halhuli (**5**). The *atabeg*, who held real power in the state of Damascus, is trying to dissuade al-Findalawi from taking part because of his great age, but the old man is insisting that he must do his duty like everyone else. Both he and al-Halhuli would be killed in the forthcoming battle.

The scene is set in one of the wider streets of the city, which is lined with tall and sometimes overhanging houses; these were made of stone for the first metre or so, and then of wooden frames with mud-brick infill and a surface of plaster above the foundations. Among the distinctive urban Damascan features that can be seen are a water-raising mill (**6**), orange trees spreading over the top of a high wall from the courtyard inside (**7**), stone-built arched doorways and passages (**8**), and flat roofs that protrude slightly beyond the walls of each building (**9**).

Quite where the commanders of the Second Crusade intended to launch their new assault is unknown, but it is likely to have been against the southern walls near the Bab al-Saghir or 'Small Gate' which, in 1148, were said to have been relatively weak and still built of mud brick. (Author's photograph)

On Sunday 25 June there was widespread and heavy fighting, the main Muslim counter-attack being north of the river. Its intention was to regain the area between the Barada and Mount Qasyun – the result being a full-scale battle somewhere between the two settlements of Upper and Lower Nayrab and the Rabwa gorge. Here the Muslims clearly suffered significant losses, including Nur al-Dawlah Shahinshah, who was Saladin's elder brother; Yusuf al-Findalawi, the *shaykh* or senior scholar of the Maliki school of Islamic law and a highly significant figure in mid-12th century Damascus; and a renowned ascetic named al-Halhuli. These losses have often led historians to assume that the Muslims were again defeated. However, there were no further references to crusaders on this northern side of the Barada and the flow of reinforcements from Lebanon now increased to such an extent that it probably tipped the balance in favour of Damascus.

In verses composed after the passing of the Second Crusade, the poet Abu'l-Hakam al-Andalusi estimates the number of casualties from the

Damascus, the Ghuta and the Barada River during the siege of July 1148

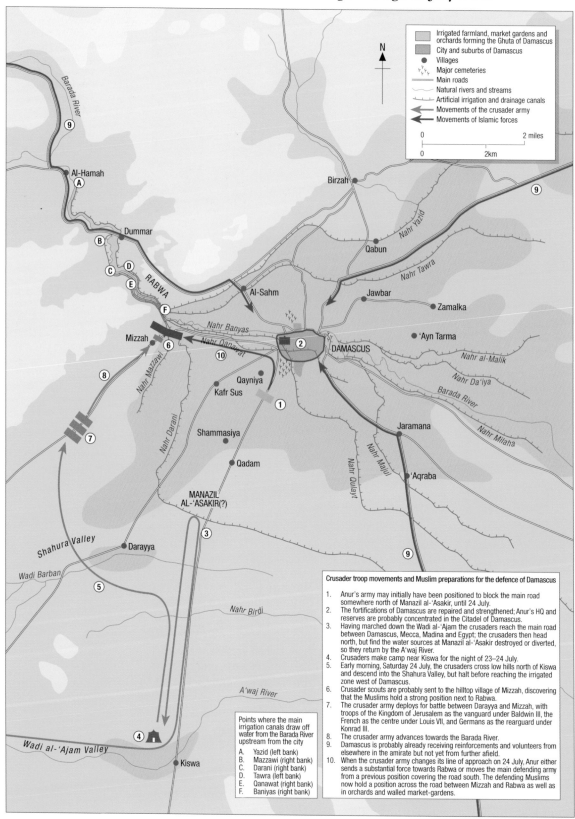

Legend:
- Irrigated farmland, market gardens and orchards forming the Ghuta of Damascus
- City and suburbs of Damascus
- ● Villages
- Major cemeteries
- Main roads
- Natural rivers and streams
- Artificial irrigation and drainage canals
- Movements of the crusader army
- Movements of Islamic forces

0 — 2 miles
0 — 2km

N

Barada River
⑨
Al-Hamah Ⓐ
Dummar Ⓑ
Ⓒ Ⓓ
Ⓔ
RABWA
Ⓕ
Nahr Banyas
Mizzah ⑥
Nahr Qanawat
⑩
⑧
Nahr Mazzawi
Qayniya
Kafr Sus ①
⑦
Nahr Darani
Shammasiya
Qadam
MANAZIL
AL-'ASAKIR(?)
③
Shahura Valley
Darayya
Wadi Barban
⑤
Nahr Birdi
A'waj River
④
Wadi al-'Ajam Valley
Kiswa

Birzah
Nahr Yazid
⑨
Qabun
Nahr Tawra
Al-Sahm
Jawbar
Zamalka
'Ayn Tarma
② DAMASCUS
Nahr al-Malik
Nahr Da'iya
Barada River
Jaramana
Nahr Milaha
Nahr Majul
Nahr Qulayt
'Aqraba
⑨

Points where the main irrigation canals draw off water from the Barada River upstream from the city

A. Yazid (left bank)
B. Mazzawi (right bank)
C. Darani (right bank)
D. Tawra (left bank)
E. Qanawat (right bank)
F. Baniyas (right bank)

Crusader troop movements and Muslim preparations for the defence of Damascus

1. Anur's army may initially have been positioned to block the main road somewhere north of Manazil al-'Asakir, until 24 July.
2. The fortifications of Damascus are repaired and strengthened; Anur's HQ and reserves are probably concentrated in the Citadel of Damascus.
3. Having marched down the Wadi al-'Ajam the crusaders reach the main road between Damascus, Mecca, Madina and Egypt; the crusaders then head north, but find the water sources at Manazil al-'Asakir destroyed or diverted, so they return by the A'waj River.
4. Crusaders make camp near Kiswa for the night of 23–24 July.
5. Early morning, Saturday 24 July, the crusaders cross low hills north of Kiswa and descend into the Shahura Valley, but halt before reaching the irrigated zone west of Damascus.
6. Crusader scouts are probably sent to the hilltop village of Mizzah, discovering that the Muslims hold a strong position next to Rabwa.
7. The crusader army deploys for battle between Darayya and Mizzah, with troops of the Kingdom of Jerusalem as the vanguard under Baldwin III, the French as the centre under Louis VII, and Germans as the rearguard under Konrad III.
8. The crusader army advances towards the Barada River.
9. Damascus is probably already receiving reinforcements and volunteers from elsewhere in the amirate but not yet from further afield.
10. When the crusader army changes its line of approach on 24 July, Anur either sends a substantial force towards Rabwa or moves the main defending army from a previous position covering the road south. The defending Muslims now hold a position across the road between Mizzah and Rabwa as well as in orchards and walled market-gardens.

This ceramic horseman was found within the walled city of Raqqa, and dates from the 12th century. His face, costume and spiral cane shield suggest that he represents a Turkish warrior, but his straight broadsword is characteristically Arab or Iranian. (National Museum, Damascus; author's photograph)

fighting as 'about 70 from Damascus' killed, together with '200 Franks and about 90 of their horses'. It is likely that he was close to the truth in these numbers. Sunday 25 July also saw fighting outside the city's al-Jabiya Gate. It is also worth noting that neither Muslim nor Christian accounts mention siege machines.

The Muslims already seem to have been engaged in guerrilla warfare in close country around the crusaders' positions, using their superior local knowledge to pick off isolated small groups or individuals. Nevertheless, the crusaders' morale remained high and they maintained their pressure upon Damascus. Indeed some of the Muslims' defensive measures were interpreted as marks of desperation, according to William of Tyre:

> In all the sections of the city which faced our camps they heaped up huge, tall beams, for they could only hope that while our men were working to tear down these barriers they might be able to flee in the opposite direction with their wives and children. (Brundage, 1976; 115–21)

This tower in the south-western wall of Damascus is almost lost within later buildings. It was said to have been the rough construction of these defences, some apparently still of mud brick, which encouraged the crusaders to consider shifting the focus of their assault. (Author's photograph)

More reinforcements poured into the city on 26 July, including peasants from the surrounding Ghuta, bedouin Arab warriors, archers from the Biqa'a Valley, bands of Turkomans and Turkish volunteers sent by Sayf al-Din Ghazi of Mosul. They arrived not only from Lebanon but also from the north-east, mostly entering Damascus through Bab Tuma and Bab Sharqi whereupon they then apparently joined the city *ahdath* militia. The defenders also launched a determined attack upon the crusaders' siege position on Monday 26 July. According to Abu Shama the Muslims even surrounded the Christians, the latter having retreated behind their palisades:

A large group of inhabitants and villagers…put to flight all the sentries, killed them, without fear of the danger, taking the heads of all the enemy they killed and wanting to touch these trophies. The number of heads they gathered was considerable. (Abu Shama, 1898; 58–59)

The following day, Tuesday 27 July, the Muslims again attacked the crusaders' siege positions. One of Sibt al-Jawzi's most colourful if garbled passages probably referred to that day and to the presence of the relic of the True Cross:

The Franks had with them a great priest with a long beard, whose teachings they obeyed. On the tenth day of their siege of Damascus [meaning the tenth day of campaign as a whole] he mounted his ass, hung a cross around his neck, took two more in his hand and hung another around the ass's neck. He had the Testaments and the crosses and the Holy Scriptures set before him and assembled the army in his presence; the only ones to remain behind were those guarding the tents. Then he said: 'The Messiah has promised me that today I will wipe out this city' … At this moment the Muslims opened the city gates and in the name of Islam charged as one man into the face of death … One of the men of the Damascus *ahdath* [militia] reached the priest, who was fighting in the front line, struck his head from his body and killed his ass too. (Gabrieli, 1969, 62–63)

THE LIFTING OF THE SIEGE

By the third day of the siege Anur knew of growing dissent amongst the enemy leadership. He may have learned that Sayf al-Din and Nur al-Din were at Hims, close enough for Anur to frighten the crusaders with the threat of Zangid intervention. In his chronicle, Ibn al-Athir gives the impression that the Zangid rulers reached Hims by 24 July. This was still five days' march from Damascus, and although Anur was probably wary of his powerful northern allies, he also knew that the crusader siege was already in trouble. Perhaps Anur exaggerated the threat of imminent Zangid intervention to further undermine crusader confidence. It is almost certain that the Zangids also sent a message to the crusader leaders, urging them to withdraw or face the combined Islamic forces.

The almost universal belief that the siege of Damascus was lifted as a result of 'betrayal' by some of the resident Frankish leadership of the crusader states probably reflected a realization amongst the local nobility that the siege could no longer succeed and that the crusaders were indeed in danger of being caught between two fires. However, the associated story that these men had been bribed by Anur of Damascus was almost certainly nonsense, while the notion that this money proved to be counterfeit was surely added to heighten the moral of the tale.

The reality was probably much more prosaic, but nevertheless leaves one of the biggest mysteries of the Second Crusade – namely the question of why and to what extent the besiegers moved their position before suddenly retreating. When news arrived concerning Nur al-Din and Sayf al-Din, the crusader leaders faced a serious strategic problem. If they remained where they were, Damascus would receive massive reinforcements within a few days while they themselves would be vulnerable to a major counter-attack. If they moved north they might prevent their enemies from joining forces but could themselves be open to attack from front and rear.

A CRUSADER SUPPLY UNIT IS AMBUSHED OUTSIDE DAMASCUS (27 JULY 1148) (pp. 72–73)

The guerrilla campaign which the defenders of Damascus launched against the Second Crusade during the latter's siege of the city achieved considerable success and may have been a major reason why the crusader leaders considered shifting the focus of their attack from the western to the southern side of Damascus. Although the siege was abandoned before that new assault took place, the fear and consternation caused by numerous guerrilla ambushes is clear in Christian accounts of the campaign.

Here a small supply unit from the German crusader army, which includes camel transport (**1**), has suddenly come under fire from both sides of one of many narrow roads through the closely packed walled gardens and orchards west of the fortified old city of Damascus. As the sources make clear, the attackers took full advantage of the available cover (**2**) and of their own detailed knowledge of the countryside. Some of the attackers can be seen charging out of the arched gateway into the orchard (**3**). During such encounters the crusaders were attacked with bows, crossbow, slings, javelins and any weapons that were available. Numerous missiles can be seen raining down on the surrounded crusaders (**4**).

A third option was to launch an immediate assault against what were thought to be weaker fortifications on the southern side of Damascus. Writing with the benefit of hindsight and perhaps confused by claims, counterclaims and excuses, William of Tyre laid the blame for this decision on the local crusader princes:

> The wall, they said, was low and was made of sunbaked bricks and it would scarcely withstand the first attack. There, they asserted, neither [siege] engines nor any great force would be needed. (Brundage, 1976; 115–21)

Mid-12th-century Arabic written descriptions and the earliest surviving maps of Damascus agree on the presence of two relatively small areas that were clear of dense cultivation or closely packed suburbs south of Damascus. One was the suburb of Qasr al-Hujjaj ('Palace of Pilgrims') where there were probably only a few buildings at the time of the Second Crusade. There was also a large market area set aside for the sale of sheep. Immediately east of the road through this area was an extensive graveyard known as the Cemetery of the Gate. However, Ibn 'Asakir makes no mention of damage being done to these areas during the crusader siege.

This third option was nevertheless taken seriously enough for the Bishop of Langres to be sent on reconnaissance. He, however, reported that the area lacked food supplies. He apparently did not mention that it was watered by the Qulayt Canal, the name given to what remained of the now polluted Baniyas which had already passed through Damascus. In the event, the crusaders never attacked the southern, still less the eastern, wall of Damascus. Nor was the proposed moving of their camp or siege position completed. Instead the invaders seem to have started their move, then realized that it could not succeed and so did little more than pause before abandoning the siege altogether. Ibn 'Asakir specifically noted that the most south-easterly point reached by the Franks was the suburb of Qayniyya, which lay south-west of the walled city. If the big move described by William of Tyre happened at all, it only got that far.

As a result, on Wednesday 28 or Thursday 29 July 1148 the huge crusader army gave up and retreated. There was naturally triumph as well as relief in Damascus. William of Tyre merely states that, 'Covered with confusion and fear, they returned to the kingdom over the same road by which they had come' (Babcock and Krey, 1976; 192), but according to Abu Shama:

> As soon as it was known that they were retreating, during the morning of the same day [29 July], the Muslims hurried to pursue them, harrassing them with arrows and killing a great number of foot soldiers, horsemen and animals amongst the slowest … The air was poisoned by the exhalations of these bodies to the extent that in much of the land it was almost impossible to breathe. (Abu Shama, 1898; 58–59)

The fighting was not over, however, and there was mutual raiding by the forces of Damascus and Jerusalem. In fact a truce between Anur, the Zangids, the Crusader States and what remained of the Second Crusade had to wait until the Christians realized that continuing the struggle was not in their interests. The biggest military operation in the aftermath of the siege of

A bronze figurine of a horseman from Iran, generally considered to have been made during the 12th or early 13th century. (Museum of Islamic Art, Cairo; author's photograph)

Communications between the *atabeg* Anur and his northern allies would have been along the road running north-eastwards from Damascus. Sentries on the walls of the citadel would certainly have been looking eagerly in this direction, watching for messengers or reinforcements. (Author's photograph)

Damascus saw another serious setback for the Crusader States in September 1148. Bertrand of Toulouse, a grandson of Raymond of Toulouse who had founded the County of Tripoli, believed that its current ruler, his cousin Count Raymond II of Tripoli, had poisoned his father soon after the Second Crusade arrived in the Middle East. Now he seized the strategic frontier castle of Arymah as the first step in taking over the County of Tripoli. Having refused to take part in the assault on Damascus, Raymond II lacked crusader allies and so sought support from his Muslim neighbours.

At the time, Anur and Nur al-Din were meeting at Ba'albak, only 80km south of Arymah. They agreed to help Count Raymond II, while Sayf al-Din, who was still at Hims, sent a contingent under a senior officer. This combined Islamic army quickly seized Arymah; Bertram of Toulouse, his sister and the surviving garrison were taken captive while Arymah's military stores were removed and the castle was dismantled.

Even so, the fighting continued and did not always go in the Zangids' favour. In September 1148 Nur al-Din began a remarkable campaign against the Principality of Antioch and the rump of the County of Edessa, which continued until the summer of 1149. It saw Nur al-Din suffer one humiliating defeat, but his army went on to conquer the Principality's remaining outposts east of the Orontes, to unsuccessfully besiege Antioch itself, and to reach the Mediterranean coast, where Nur al-Din saw the sea for the first time in his life. Eventually he and the Prince of Antioch agreed a truce that established a new frontier for the now truncated principality; the strategic fortress of Harim remained in Muslim hands while the territory west of the castle was returned to the Franks.

Mindful of Nur al-Din's support during the siege of Damascus, not to mention the fact that the Zangid rulers of Aleppo and Mosul were considerably more powerful than Damascus, Anur had supported Nur al-Din with a substantial military contingent during this campaign. Meanwhile Konrad III had gone home on 8 September 1148, disappointed by the lack of support for his suggestion that the crusader forces achieve something for all their efforts, but driving the Fatimid garrison out of Ascalon. He sailed to Thessaloniki where he accepted the Emperor Manuel's invitation to spend the winter in Constantinople. Leaving the Byzantine capital in February 1149, Konrad reached Germany in spring while Manuel went to supervise the Byzantine siege of Siculo-Norman-held Corfu.

Most French commanders of the Second Crusade returned to France during the late summer and autumn of 1148, but King Louis and his increasingly estranged wife Eleanor celebrated Christmas and Easter in the Holy Land, despite Abbot Suger's pleas for Louis to come home. Finally, in late April 1149, they boarded separate Sicilian ships and headed for the Norman Kingdom of Sicily. After an extraordinarily eventful journey Louis VII finally returned to France some time in November 1149.

Back in Syria, the *atabeg* Anur's truce with the Kingdom of Jerusalem was clearly to the advantage of Damascus. What Damascus got from its continuing alliance with Nur al-Din of Aleppo, however, was the temporary removal of a threat to its continuing independence. Anur died on 28 August 1149, one year and one month after the defeat of the Second Crusade's siege of Damascus. Just under five years later, in April 1154, it would be Nur al-Din – not the Franks – who finally took control of that ancient city and its principality.

AFTERMATH

The impact of the Second Crusade was wide-ranging, though Islamic chroniclers who were not based in Damascus itself generally regarded these events as being of secondary importance compared with what was happening in Iraq and western Iran. Here the focus of attention was upon the decline of the Great Saljuq Sultanate and the revival of the 'Abbasid Caliphate as a temporal power as well as a religious authority. Even in cultural and religious terms it was not until after the Second Crusade that jihad became a major aspect of Islamic civilization in the Middle East.

The principality of Damascus had survived and its relations with the powerful Zangid states of Aleppo and Mosul remained harmonious until the death of the *atabeg* Anur. The young prince Abaq now took over. Though his authority had previously been nominal, he was in many ways the old *atabeg*'s pupil. However, just over two months after the death of Anur a power struggle broke out between prince Abaq and the *ra'is*, civilian 'mayor' and commander of the powerful *ahdath* militia Mu'ayyad al-Dawlah Ibn al-Sufi. With his brother Haidar he mustered many of the *ahdath* and instigated a rebellion. The *ahdath* had, of course, done much to defeat the Second Crusade's siege and may even have felt that it deserved more credit.

There followed a period of political infighting and disturbance, which, although it does not seem to have been aimed at toppling Prince Abaq himself, offered Nur al-Din an opportunity to intervene in Damascene affairs. When Abaq refused to send troops to support another of Nur al-Din's campaigns against crusader territory, the ruler of Aleppo attacked Damascus instead. This assault in 1150 was hampered by heavy rain, but nevertheless Abaq recognized Nur al-Din's military strength and so agreed to have his rival's name mentioned in Friday prayers. This symbolic act had, throughout Islamic history, been a means whereby the superior authority of a ruler was recognized. The following year Nur al-Din again appeared outside the walls of Damascus, but instead of attacking he ordered his men to harvest the surrounding crops, causing higher prices and economic hardship within the city. An attempt by King Baldwin of Jerusalem to intervene came to nothing. For the next few years Nur al-Din increased the pressure, largely by economic means. Then, in March 1154 he sent an army to attack the city directly. The following month he himself joined the siege and in April Abaq Ibn Muhammad Abu Sa'id Mujir al-Din, the last Burid ruler of Damascus, handed over his city and left for Hims, where he was granted an *'iqta* or fief.

The decades following the defeat of the Second Crusade saw a steady increase in the influence of Sunni Muslims in Damascus, with a parallel

decline in the Shi'a. Shaykh Yusuf Ibn Dunas Abu'l-Hajjah al-Findalawi, as a hero not only of the fight against the crusaders but also as a leading figure in the Sunni community, was widely regarded as one of the campaign's most important 'martyrs'. Meanwhile, the impact of the Second Crusade upon the Zangid rulers was less than it was upon Damascus. The senior member of the family, Sayf al-Din Ghazi I Ibn Zangi of Mosul, died the following year, being succeeded as ruler of Mosul by another of his brothers, Qutb al-Din Mawdud Ibn Zangi whose long rule would last until 1170. Meanwhile Nur al-Din Mahmud Ibn Zangi continued to reign in Aleppo, and subsequently also in Damascus, until his death in 1174.

Beyond these dramatic military and political events, the decades following the Second Crusade saw a shift in the centre of gravity of Islamic cultural life away from the old centres in central Iraq and Iran to the Zangid states. Under Saladin and his successors, Cairo would join Damascus, Aleppo and Mosul as the cultural powerhouses of the Islamic Middle East.

Within 20 years of the debacle of the Second Crusade, the Isma'ilis had established a small, independent and remarkable formidable state in the northern coastal mountains of Syria. Generally known to Western historians as the 'Assassin's State', it would play a significant part in the continuing history of the Crusades in the Middle East. In the long run, events in Anatolia were of greater significance, especially to European history. Here the people and state now known as Turkey were in the process of being created, while the Saljuq Sultanate of Rum was moving from the 'heroic age' of conquest and survival to a remarkable flowering of culture as well as increasing economic wealth.

One of the most important unknown factors in the history of the Second Crusade is when the armies of Nur al-Din of Aleppo and Sayf al-Din of Mosul reached the fortified city of Hims in central Syria. Its fortifications were restored and strengthened by Nur al-Din in 565 AH (AD 1169–70) following severe earthquake damage. (Author's photograph)

Within Europe the failure of the Second Crusade's primary objective of supporting the Latin States in the Holy Land does not seem to have undermined enthusiasm for crusading, at least not amongst those most directly involved. Other efforts were soon made, or at least attempted. As early as 1149–50 King Loius VII of France and King Roger II attempted to form an alliance against the Byzantine Emperor Manuel, whom they blamed for the failure of the Second Crusade. This was an astonishing claim on the part of Roger, who had tried to use the passage of the crusaders through Byzantine territory to further his own ambitions in Greece and the western Balkans. The proposal never got off the ground, however, because the German Emperor Konrad III refused to break his links with Manuel.

Failure was, nevertheless, difficult for the military aristocracies of Western and Central Europe to accept. In fact the 'West' was already demonstrating a tendency to seize on any excuse to explain military defeat at the hands of a Muslim people. It was then, as now, easier to blame others and this was probably why the idea that the Second Crusade had been betrayed by 'Syrian Franks', the resident colonial aristocracy of the Crusader States, was so widely and so rapidly believed.

Amongst a few scholars, churchmen and literary figures there was, meanwhile, a strengthening belief that the Crusades did not have divine approval, and that this accounted for the Second Crusade's failure. Bernard of Clairvaux himself wrestled with this problem and almost seemed to criticize God's good sense:

> Clearly the Lord, provoked by our sins, seems in some way to have judged the earth before an appointed time, rightly of course, but unmindful of his mercy. He neither spared his people, nor his own name. Are they not saying among the nations, 'Where is their God?' (Switten, in Gervers, 1991; 75)

Within the crusader Kingdom of Jerusalem, William of Tyre sadly summed up the effect of Second Crusade:

> They departed [i.e. set out] under unlucky auspices, however, and with sinister omens. For they started on the way as if contrary to the will of an angry God, and, in punishment for the sins of man. They accomplished nothing pleasing to Him on that entire pilgrimage. Nay, they even rendered worse the situation of those to whom they intended to bring succor. (Babcock and Krey, 1976; 165)

Because medieval chroniclers normally only provided detailed information about the fate of individuals if the latter were members of the aristocratic or clerical elite, not much is known about what happened to the majority of those who fought during the Second Crusade. Of the 113 named individuals who are known to have taken part on the Christian side, 22 certainly died, 42 are known to have returned home while the fate of the remaining 49 remains a mystery. One of the few sources to shed light on the fate of those who were captured is the anonymous writer of the *Annales Herbipolenses* from Würzburg in Germany. Of particular interest is his statement that he met many returned soldiers who had been captured by the Turks in Anatolia and later released. Various, sometimes obscure, sources indicate that the Armenians were largely instrumental in ransoming, or arranging the ransoming, of these crusaders.

A Saljuq Turkish prince surrounded by his guards and perhaps his senior military commanders, as illustrated on a late 12th- or early 13th-century painted plate from Iran. (Museum of Fine Arts, inv. 63.1386, Boston)

The Crusader States were now practically exhausted, militarily and financially, so it is hardly surprising that, from the mid-12th century onwards, their original warlike zeal was replaced by a cautious determination to survive. The individual Crusader States also seemed to be losing their early spirit of cooperation. In 1152, two years after the last remnant of the County of Edessa fell to Nur al-Din, Count Raymond II of Tripoli was assassinated, being succeeded by Raymond III. At Easter that year King Baldwin III forced his mother, Queen Melisende, to abdicate as co-ruler, finally enabling him to become the undisputed ruler of the Kingdom of Jerusalem. Then, on 22 August 1153, the crusader kingdom achieved what could be seen as its last real territorial victory when the Fatimid outpost of Ascalon finally surrendered after a prolonged blockade and a nine-month siege. Despite unsubstantiated criticism of the way in which the Military Order of Templars supposedly accepted a bribe from the enemy during the siege of Damascus, their reputation as a fighting force continued to grow. Meanwhile, for reasons that remain unknown, no criticism was directed towards the actions of their rivals, the Hospitallers, during the Second Crusade.

Because Konrad III and the German Empire played such a leading role in the Second Crusade, this was where its failure was felt most deeply. Otto of Freising summed up the feelings of those who tried to put a positive gloss on the whole sorry affair: 'If our expedition was not good for the extension of boundaries or the comfort of our bodies, it was good, however, for the salvation of many souls.' Other chroniclers were brutally direct in their criticism, Gerhoh of Reichersberg maintaining that the entire expedition had been inspired by the devil. The anonymous author of the *Annales*

The aftermath of the Second Crusade, 29 July 1148–August 1149

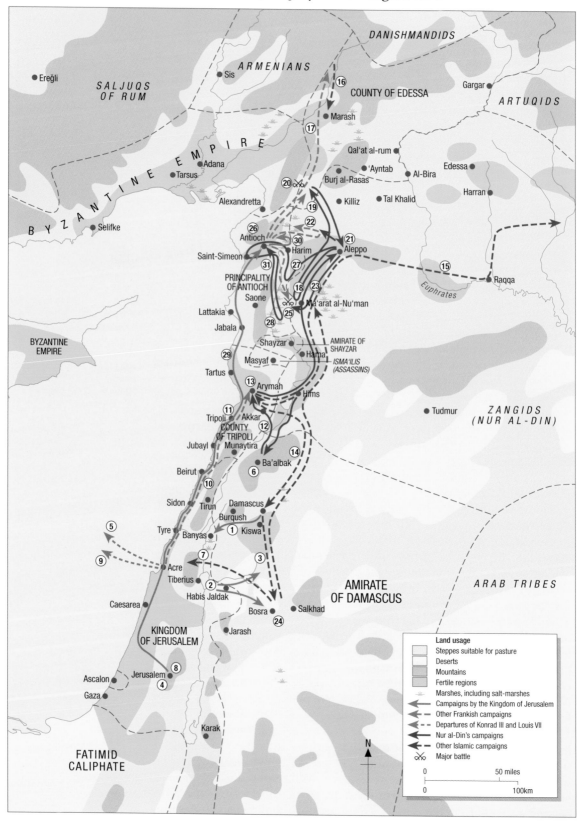

Ereğli

SALJUQS
OF RUM

DANISHMANDIDS

Sis
ARMENIANS
COUNTY OF EDESSA
Gargar
ARTUQIDS

(16)
Marash
(17)

Qal'at al-rum
'Ayntab
Al-Bira
Edessa

Adana
Tarsus

BYZANTINE EMPIRE

Burj al-Rasas
Killiz
Tal Khalid
Harran

Alexandretta

(20)
(19)
(22)

Selifke

(26)
Antioch
Saint-Simeon
(30) Harim
(31)
(27)
(21) Aleppo

(15)
Raqqa
Euphrates

PRINCIPALITY
OF ANTIOCH
Saone
(18) (23)
(25)
Ma'arat al-Nu'man

Lattakia
Jabala
(28)

AMIRATE OF
SHAYZAR

BYZANTINE
EMPIRE

Shayzar
Masyaf
Hama
ISMA'ILIS
(ASSASSINS)

(29)
Tartus
(13) Arymah
Hims

Tudmur
ZANGIDS
(NUR AL-DIN)

(11)
Tripoli Akkar
COUNTY
OF TRIPOLI
(12)
Jubayl Munaytira
(14)
Ba'albak
(6)

Beirut
(10)
Sidon Tirun
Damascus
Burqush
(5)
(1) Kiswa
Tyre Banyas
(9)
(7)
(3)
Acre
Tiberius
(2)
Habis Jaldak
Caesarea
Bosra Salkhad
(24)
Jarash

AMIRATE
OF DAMASCUS

ARAB TRIBES

KINGDOM
OF JERUSALEM

(8)
Ascalon Jerusalem
(4)
Gaza

Karak

FATIMID
CALIPHATE

N

Land usage
Steppes suitable for pasture
Deserts
Mountains
Fertile regions
Marshes, including salt-marshes
Campaigns by the Kingdom of Jerusalem
Other Frankish campaigns
Departures of Konrad III and Louis VII
Nur al-Din's campaigns
Other Islamic campaigns
Major battle

0   50 miles
0   100km

Herbipolenses of Würzburg went as far as to describe its preachers as 'pseudo-prophets, sons of Belial, heads of anti-Christ'.

In more practical terms, Konrad III and his nephew, the future emperor Frederick Barbarossa, returned from the Second Crusade to find there had been a notable increase in local violence in Germany. Konrad did what he could to re-establish law and order, but he still left a difficult situation to his successor Frederick, who came to the throne in 1152.

The cultural impact within German-speaking Europe was obscured by a general desire to forget an embarrassing episode. Nevertheless, enough members of the knightly elite returned with personal experiences, which fed into the literature of following decades. Thus, it has been suggested that some descriptions of battles between Christians and Saracens in Wolfram's epic poem *Willehalm*, written around 1170, echo events in the Second Crusade. Despite its brutality, this epic is also characterized by a remarkably high regard for the courage, determination and noble behaviour of the Saracen foes.

The failure of the Second Crusade similarly led to a temporary decline in enthusiasm for crusading in much of France. Nevertheless, King Louis suffered less direct criticism than Konrad for his leadership of the campaign, which clearly did not undermine his prestige. Indeed his piety and willingness to accept tribulations and defeats with devout resignation led Louis VII to be seen as a pilgrim rather than a crusader. Nor was Louis's enthusiasm for religious pilgrimage, as distinct from warlike crusading, dulled by his experiences in the Holy Land. Only a few years after returning from Jerusalem he visited the increasingly important pilgrimage centre of Santiago de Compostela in north-western Spain.

The impact of the Second Crusade was more obvious in medieval French culture than in German. Nevertheless, it was the story of Queen Eleanor's supposed affair with Prince Raymond that caught the attention of poets and troubadours, especially in the Occitan-speaking south and west of France. The crusader Principality of Antioch also seems to have become a centre of troubadour literature, the epic *Chanson des Chétifs* being written in Raymond's court shortly before 1149. The original version does not survive, but a later 12th- or early 13th-century reworking of the *Chanson des Chétifs* by Graindor de Douai would be integrated into the *First Crusade Cycle*.

In England there was a natural tendency to contrast the success of the siege of Lisbon with the failure of that of Damascus. Henry of Huntingdon ascribed an absence of God's grace at the aristocratic siege of Damascus, whereas in his view God had been with the lowly crusaders in Portugal. He also took a clear pride in the fact that a large proportion of these men had come from England. In southern Italy the Norman Kingdom of Sicily took advantage of these war-torn years to extend its authority, and although King Roger II's campaign against the Byzantine Empire failed, the Siculo-Norman fleet's capture of the Tunisian coastal city of Mahdia in 1148 resulted in a brief period of Norman rule. King Roger II's huge ambitions were, in fact, expressed in the words inscribed on the blade of his sword: 'The Apulian and the Calabrian, the Sicilian and the African serve me.'

The impact of the Second Crusade upon the Byzantine Empire was largely negative. Relations between the Byzantines and the French were damaged, with King Louis, Bishop Odo and other French leaders eventually coming to the conclusion that the Emperor Manuel had encouraged Turkish attacks upon them as they marched across Anatolia. Almost as ominous for the future of the Byzantine Empire was Bishop Odo of Deuil's expressed opinion that the fortifications of Constantinople were not as strong as commonly believed. The largely French Fourth Crusade would, in fact, attack and overrun the Byzantine Imperial capital just over half a century later.

If crusader accusations of collusion with the Turks are largely unfounded, the Byzantine authorities certainly used their renowned political skills to deal with the perceived threat posed by the Second Crusade. This is clearly expressed in a subsequent eulogy for the Emperor Manuel, written by Archbishop Eustathios of Thessalonika who highlighted the emperor's success in dealing with the sudden arrival of two major armies from Western Europe:

[He] was able to deal with his enemies with enviable skill, playing off one against the other with the aim of bringing about peace and tranquility. (Harris, 2003; 95)

Militarily, the Byzantine Empire seemed to be strong in the immediate aftermath of the Second Crusade, having contained the crusader armies, defeated the Siculo-Normans and the Kipchaq Turks. The Byzantine fleet had reached one of its peaks, but thereafter steadily declined. On land the Emperor Manuel ordered the construction of another series of castles to protect the region around Adramyttion (Edremit), Pergamon (Bergama) and Chliara (Kirkagaç) in western Anatolia. This was a success, but remained

Figures representing members of the Muslim ruling elite, courtiers or guardsmen were found in various forms of decoration during this period, even being moulded onto everyday objects like this large earthenware storage jar from Mosul. (National Museum, Damascus; author's photograph)

limited in its scope. In many other parts of nominally Byzantine Anatolia, the Greek-speaking Christian population continued to decline. At Ephesus, where the French and German armies of the Second Crusade had spent the Christmas of 1147, the population gradually moved away from the ancient city near the river and now largely silted-up harbour to the fortified hilltop town now called Ayasoluk. Today the site is dominated by a magnificent, largely 13th-century Byzantine fortress. Even so the old 'lower town' with its extensive ancient and early Christian ruins was finally abandoned by the Turkish conquest of 1304.

During the late 11th and 12th century Byzantine reconquest of western Anatolia, many of the Turkish chiefs remained in this area, even after being defeated by the emperors Alexius, John or Manuel, converting to Christianty along with their tribes and now fighting for Byzantium. There was also clearly considerable intermarriage between Greeks and Turks both during and after this period. It was a process that would later have a profound impact on Anatolian Islam, the great majority of the Anatolian population converting once again and taking a wide range of Christian practices and beliefs with them, some orthodox Christian and others distinctly unorthodox.

The Leaning Minaret of the Jami al-Kabir or Great Mosque in Mosul was built by Nur al-Din between 1170 and 1172, as part of major alterations to the mosque built by his brother Sayf al-Din in celebration of the defeat of the Second Crusade. (Author's photograph)

Away to the south-east in Cilicia, the Byzantine authorities do not at first seem to have taken the Armenian threat very seriously. Preoccupied with the approach of the Second Crusade and the Siculo-Norman invasion, the government in Constantinople failed to react, and by 1150 almost all of Cilicia was in Armenian hands under the new ruler of Armenian Cilicia, King Toros II. In 1152 the Byzantine Emperor Manuel sent an army commanded by his cousin Andronicus, the future emperor. However, after achieving a few initial successes, Andronicus was defeated by Toros and several of the Byzantines' most important Armenian allies were captured.

Across the mountains in what had been the crusader County of Edessa stood the fortress known as Ranculat by the Franks, Qal'at al-Rum in Arabic,

Horomkla by the Armenians and now Rum Kalesi by the Turks. It overlooked the upper Euphrates and, in 1150 it remained one of a handful of outposts still held by Countess Beatrice of Edessa in the Euphrates region. While the others were sold to the Byzantines who were currently trying to reconquer Cilicia, Ranculat was instead given by the countess to the Armenian Catholicos, the most senior figure in the Armenian church hierarchy in this part of the Middle East. A nearby Armenian frontier baron and vassal of the Muslim Turkish Artuqid dynasties, Vasil Pahlawouni of Karkar, similarly insisted that the Armenian Catholicos transfer his official residence to the fortress of Ranculat in 1150. As it happened, the Byzantine campaign in Cilicia was a failure, and the revived Armenian kingdom never spread its authority this far east. As a result, the fortress of Rum Kalesi remained the residence of the Armenian Catholicos under Turkish rule for a further one and a half centuries.

The Second Crusade never caught the attention and imagination of the modern Western world in the way that the First, Third and even Fourth Crusades would do. One of the few to look at this remarkable campaign in a broader historical light was the German philosopher Nietzsche who drew parallels between the failure of the Second Crusade and the defeat of Napoleon's Grand Army in Russia in 1812. In broader cultural terms, the French troubadour Jaufré Rudel, who personally took part in the Second Crusade, would have huge influence upon 19th-century Romanticism. More recently, his life formed the subject of an opera by the Finnish composer Kaija Saariaho, the libretto being written by an Arab scholar of the Crusades, Amin Maalouf. The piece was premiered in 2000.

THE BATTLEFIELDS TODAY

Like the First Crusade, the Second involved several expeditions from Western Europe, most of which had to fight their way to the Middle East. Consequently, there were several 'battlefields' in addition to the siege of Damascus itself. Even after the failure of that siege, one further confrontation – the loss of al-Uraymah to Nur al-Din – must be included in the overall story of the Second Crusade.

Those who want to follow in the footsteps of the main land contingents will find that their routes are traced by good modern roads while the major cities along the way can also be reached by rail. Only when the routes reach Anatolia in what is now Asiatic Turkey does the journey become more difficult. King Konrad III and the German contingent pressed on after passing Eskisehir (Dorylaeum), heading for Konya along what is now the main road towards Ankara. They then veered south-east along what is now a metalled but secondary road towards Aksehir. How far they reached is unknown, but it seems likely that they were forced to turn back before reaching Emirdag. This part of Central Anatolia is not visited by many tourists, unlike Cappadocia farther east, so its hotel facilities are limited. Apart from a few expensive hotels, most largely seem to cater for long-distance lorry drivers.

The more westerly routes followed by the French contingent, and by the Germans after their defeat beyond Eskisehir, are a mixture of well-trodden tourist paths and relatively short stretches of more difficult road. For example, the first part of their route to the Aegean coast is now a good if winding road via Balikesir, through a fertile region with adequate small hotels. Once the coast is reached near Edremit, the route runs through a major tourist zone, pleasant in many places, considerably overdeveloped in others, but with abundant hotels in all price ranges. The modern road, like the medieval one, does not always follow the coast, but it is only after Izmir (Smyrna) that it winds inland away from a coast that is being developed as a major tourist destination. The classical and early Christian ruins of Efes, the ancient Ephesus, are also an important visitor attraction.

Between Efes and Antalya the going gets more difficult, though in recent years the whole route has reportedly been given a proper tarmac surface. The French crusaders fought three battles during this relatively short section of their journey: the first at an unknown spot in the fertile Menderes (Meander) Valley, the second close to the summit of the still difficult Kazik Beli Pass just beyond Denizli and the third probably at a double-crossing of the upper Dalaman River just beyond Acipayam. This is still an underdeveloped part of Turkey where tourist facilities are limited.

Once the Mediterranean coast is reached at Antalya, the roads are good and all forms of tourist facilities abound. How many of Louis VII's troops managed to continue along the coast to rejoin their king at Antakya (Antioch) is unknown. However, the traveller wishing to rejoin the route of the main contingents of the Second Crusade can easily follow a long, winding but well-maintained and picturesque road along Turkey's Mediterranean coast. The route then cuts inland across the fertile but somewhat featureless province of Cilicia before turning south into the Hatay province and across the mountains to Antakya itself. Though on the fringes of what might be regarded as Turkey's main tourist regions, Anatakya is a fascinating city, partially Syrian-Arab in culture, with excellent facilities and an abundance of historical sites, not least the partially crusader citadel at the highest point of the extensive city walls.

As far as the crusaders were concerned, the rest of their campaign took place within what are now Syria, Lebanon and Palestine–Israel. King Louis of France and many of his fellow crusaders made a point of visiting the main Christian holy places in Palestine. These are currently within Israel and the occupied Palestinian territory generally known as the West Bank. The Second Crusade's march to Damascus also went across the Golan Heights. Until recently, many historians have assumed that the massive castle of Subayba was the fortress of Banyas. In fact, the Banyas that changed hands so often during the 12th century, and in which the crusaders stopped for local advice, was the little Syrian frontier town still called Banyas. Nearby Subayba dates from the 13th century and is an entirely Islamic fortress. The old road from Banyas to Damascus remains closed. A visitor who wishes to travel to both Israel and Syria has to enter each country separately and will require two passports.

Before looking at Damascus itself, which is one of the truly great cities of the Middle East, mention should be made of Lebanon. Not only did many of the troops who tipped the balance in favour of Damascus come from the

King Roger II, the Norman ruler of Sicily and southern Italy, took advantage of the Second Crusade to invade the western provinces of the Byzantine Empire. In this manuscript illustration made around 1150 he appears with his guards – one Christian and one Muslim. (*Regestum di Sant Angelo in Formis*, Ms. Reg. 4, Library of the Abbey of Monte Cassino)

Biqa'a Valley and neighbouring hills, but the ancient city of Ba'albak featured prominently in these events. It is certainly worth visiting, not least for the magnificent Roman temple complex which served as a citadel during the medieval period.

Travel to and within Syria is easy, the roads are good, car hire is cheap, and the facilities are excellent and spread across the whole country. However, it remains an unfortunate fact that most of the locations directly associated with the 1148 siege of Damascus are now covered by the expanding, occasionally chaotic, noisy but bustling and friendly Syrian capital – the only major exception being the walled Old City itself. Fortunately the Syrians' love of green spaces, added to the cultural and town-planning influence of France, means that little of Damascus can be described as a concrete jungle. Nevertheless, Tishrin Park in the west and the small farms which come almost up to the eastern wall of the Old City still give some idea of the lush surroundings of medieval Damascus. The entire walled city has itself been designated by UNESCO as a World Heritage Site and, with a few unfortunate exceptions, its character and buildings are preserved by very strict architectural and planning regulations.

FURTHER READING

Abu Shama, 'Kitab al-Rawdatayn', in *Recueil des Historiens des Croisades: Historiens Orientaux*, vols. 4 & 5 (Paris, 1898)

Amedroz, H.F., 'Three Arabic MSS. on the History of the City of Mayyafariqin', *Journal of the Royal Asiatic Society*, 34 (1902), pp. 785–812

Anon. (tr. J.C. Meisami), *Bahr al-Fawa'id: the Sea of Precious Virtues* (Salt Lake City, 1991). Includes text on jihad, written in 12th–13th-century Syria.

Arnold, B., *German Knighthood 1050–1300* (Oxford, 1985)

Azhari, T.K. el-, *The Saljuqs of Syria during the Crusades 463–549 A.H./1070–1154 AD* (Berlin, 1997)

Bar Hebraeus (tr. E.W. Budge), *The Chronology of Gregory Abu'l Farag, Commonly Known as Bar Hebraeus* (London, 1932)

Bédier, J., and P. Aubry, *Les Chansons de Croisade avec leur Mélodies* (Geneva, 1974)

Beech, G.T., 'The crusader Lordship of Marash in Armenian Cilicia, 1104–1149', *Viator*, 28 (1996), pp. 35–52

Bombaci, A., 'The Army of the Saljuqs of Rum', *Istituto Orientale di Napoli, Annali*, 38 (1978), pp. 343–69

Braune, M., 'Die Stadtmauer von Damaskus', *Damaszener Mitteilungen*, 11 (1999), pp. 67–88 and plates 13–14

Brundage, J.A (tr.), *The Crusades: a Documentary Survey* (Milwaukee, 1976)

Bull, M., 'The Capetian Monarchy and the Early Crusade Movement: Hugh of Vermandois and Louis VII', *Nottingham Medieval Studies*, 40 (1996), pp.25-46

Bull, M.G., and C. Leglu (eds.), *The World of Eleanor of Aquitaine: Literature and Society in Southern France between the Eleventh and Thirteenth Centuries* (Woodbridge, 2005)

Cole, P.J., *The Preaching of the Crusades to the Holy Land, 1095–1270* (Cambridge, MA, 1991)

Constable, G., 'A Note on the Route of the Anglo-Flemish crusaders of 1147', *Speculum*, 28 (1953), pp. 525–26

—— 'The Financing of the Crusades in the Twelfth century', in B.Z. Kedar (ed.), *Outremer: Studies in the History of the Crusading Kingdom of Jerusalem* (Jerusalem, 1982), pp. 64–88

——'The Second Crusade as seen by Contemporaries', *Traditio*, 9 (1953), pp. 213–79

Dadoyan, S.B., *The Fatimid Armenians: Culture and Political Interaction in the Middle East* (Leiden, 1997)

Dajani-Shakeel, H., 'Diplomatic Relations between Muslim and Frankish Rulers 1097–1153 AD', in M. Shatzmiller (ed.), *Crusaders and Muslims in Twelfth-Century Syria* (Leiden, 1993), pp. 190–215

Dédéyan, G., 'Razzias 'Turcomanes' et contre-razzias Arméniennes dans le Diyâr Bakr au début du XIIe siècle…', in R. Curiel and R. Gyselen (eds.), *Itinéraires d'Orient: Hommages à Claude Cahen* (Bures-sur-Yvette, 1994), pp. 49–58

—— 'Un émir arménien de Hawrân entre la principauté turque de Damas et le royaume latin de Jérusalem (1147)', in M. Balard (ed.), *Dei gesta per Francos* (Aldershot, 2001), pp. 179–85

Eidelberg, S. (ed. and tr.), *Jews and Crusaders: the Hebrew Chronicles of the First and Second Crusades* (Madison, 1977)

Elisseeff, N., *La description de Damas d'Ibn 'Asakir* (Damascus, 1959)

—— *Nur al-Din: un Grand Prince Musulman de Syrie au Temps des Croisades* (Damascus, 1967)

Fawtier, R. (tr. L. Butler and R.J. Adam), *The Capetian Kings of France: Monarchy and Nation (987–1328)*, (London, 1960)

Fink, H.S., 'The Role of Damascus in the History of the Crusades', *Muslim World*, 40 (1950), pp. 41–53

Forey, A.J., 'The Failure of the siege of Damascus in 1148', *Journal of Medieval History*, 10 (1984), pp. 13–23

France, J., 'Logistics and the Second Crusade', in J.H. Pryor (ed.), *Logistics of Warfare in the Age of the Crusades* (Aldershot, 2006), pp. 77–94

Gabrieli, F. (tr.), *Arab Historians of the Crusades* (London, 1969)

Gerish, D., 'The True Cross and the Kings of Jerusalem', *Journal of the Haskins Society*, 8 (1996), pp. 137–55

Gervers, M. (ed.) *The Second Crusade and the Cistercians* (New York, 1991)

Grabois, A., 'The Crusade of King Louis VII: a Reconsideration', in P.W. Edbury (ed.), *Crusade and Settlement* (Cardiff, 1985), pp. 94–104

Hampe, K. (tr. R. Bennet), *Germany under the Salian and Hohenstaufen Emperors* (Oxford, 1973)

Hanisch, H., 'Die seldschukischen Zitadelle von Damaskus', *Damaszener Mitteilungen*, 6 (1992), pp. 479–99 and plates 79–82

Harris, J., *Byzantium and the Crusades* (London, 2003)

Hillenbrand, C., *A Muslim Principality in Crusader Times: Tarikh Mayyafariqin* (partial trans. of Ibn al-Azraq) (Leiden, 1990)

Hoch, M., 'The Choice of Damascus as the Objective of the Second Crusade; a Re-evaluation', in M. Balard (ed.), *Autour de la Première Croisade* (Paris, 1996) pp. 359–69

Ibn al-Qalanisi (tr. H.A.R. Gibb), *The Damascus Chronicle of the Crusades* (London, 1932; reprint London, 1967)

—— (tr. R. Le Tourneau), *Damas de 1075 á 1154: traduction annotée d'un fragment de l'histoire de Damas d'Ibn al-Qalanisi* (Damascus, 1952)

Jubb, M., 'Enemies in the Holy War, but brothers in chivalry: the crusaders' view of their Saracen opponents', in H. Van Dijk (ed.), *Aspects de l'épopée romane: mentalités, idéologies, intertextualités* (Groningen, 1995), pp. 251–59

Kelly, A., *Eleanor of Aquitaine and the Four Kings* (Cambridge, MA, 1950)

Kinnamos, J. (tr. C.M. Brand), *The Deeds of John and Manuel Comnenus by John Kinnamos* (New York, 1976)

La Monte, J.L., *Feudal Monarchy in the Latin Kingdom of Jerusalem* (Cambridge, MA, 1932)

Leclerq, J., 'L'attitude spirituelle de S. Barnard devant la guerre', *Collectanéa Cisterciensis*, 36 (1974), pp. 195–225

Lewis, A.R., 'Northern European Sea Power and the Straits of Gibraltar, 1031–1350 AD', in W.C. Jordan et al. (eds.), *Order and Innovation in the Middle Ages: Essays in Honor of Joseph R. Strayer* (Princeton, 1976), pp. 139–64

Leyser, K.J., *Medieval Germany and its Neighbours* (London, 1982)

Libertini, C.G., 'Practical Crusading: the transformation of Crusading practice 1095–1221', in M. Balard (ed.), *Autour de la Première Croisade* (Paris, 1996), pp. 281–91

Lillie, R-J., (tr. J.C. Morris and J.E. Ridings), *Byzantium and the Crusader States 1096–1204* (Oxford, 1993)

Loud, G.A., 'Some Reflections on the Failure of the Second Crusade', *Crusades*, 4 (2005), pp. 1–14

Luchaire, A., *Études sur les Actes de Louis VII* (Paris, 1885)

Mayer, H.E., 'The Crusader Principality of Galilee between Saint-Omer and Bures-sur-Yvette', in R. Curiel and R. Gyselen (eds.), *Itinéraires d'Orient: Hommages à Claude Cahen* (Bures-sur-Yvette, 1994), pp. 157–67

Mayer. H.E., 'The Wheel of Fortune: Seigneurial Vicissitudes under Kings Fulk and Balwin III of Jerusalem', *Speculum*, 65 (1990), pp. 860–77

Mentgen, G., 'Kreuzzüge und Judenpogrome', in H-J. Kotzur (ed.), *Kein Krieg ist Heilig: Die Kreuzzüge* (Mainz, 2004), pp. 65–75

Mirza, N.A., *Syrian Isma'ilism* (London, 1997)

Mouton, J-M., 'Yusuf al-Fandalawi, cheikh des malikites de Damas sous les Bourides', *Revue des Études Islamiques*, 51 (1983), pp. 63–75

Mouton, J-M., *Damas et sa principauté sous les Seljoukides et les Bourides 468–549/1076–1154* (Cairo, 1994)

Murray, A.V., 'Galilee and Damascus in the period of the Crusades', *Nottingham Medieval Studies*, 40 (1996), pp. 190–93

Nickerson, M.E., 'The seigneury of Beirut in the Twelfth Century', *Byzantion*, 19 (1949), pp. 141–85

Nicolle, D., *Crusader Warfare* (2 vols.) (London, 2007)

Otto of Freising (tr. C.C. Mierow and R. Emery), *The Deeds of Frederick Barbarossa by Otto of Freising and his Continuator, Rahewin* (New York, 1953)

Phillips, J.P., *The Second Crusade: Extending the Frontiers of Christendom* (New Haven, 2007)

Phillips, J.P., and M. Hoch (eds.), *The Second Crusade: Scope and Consequences* (Manchester, 2001)

—— *Defenders of the Holy Land: Relations between the Latin East and the West, 1119–1187* (Oxford, 1996)

—— 'The Murder of Charles the Good and the Second Crusade: Household Nobility and the Traditions of Crusading in Medieval Flanders', *Medieval Prosopography*, 19 (1998), pp. 55–75

Rassow, P., 'Zum byzantinische-normanischen Krieg 1147–49', *Mitteilungen des Institüts für Osterreichische Geschichtsforschung*, 62 (1954), pp. 213–18

Rheinheimer, M., *Das Kreuzfahrerfürstentum Galiläa* (Kiel, 1990)

Richard, J., 'Le siège de Damas dans l'histoire et la légende', in M. Goodrich (ed.), *Cross-cultural convergences in the crusader period: essays presented to Aryeh Grabois on his sixty-fifth birthday* (New York, 1995), pp. 225–35

Roche, J.T., 'Conrad III and the Second Crusade; Retreat from Dorylaion', *Crusades*, 5 (2006), pp. 85–98

Rogers, R., *Latin Siege Warfare in the Twelfth Century* (Oxford, 1992)

Salibi, K.S., 'The Maronites of Lebanon under Frankish and Mamluk Rule (1099–1516)', *Arabica*, 4 (1957), pp. 288–303

—— *Maronite Historians of the Medieval Lebanon* (Beirut, 1959; reprint Beirut, 1991)

Sayar. I.M., 'The Empire of the Salcuqids of Asia Minor', *Journal of Near Eastern Studies*, 10 (1951), pp. 268–80

Sesan, M., 'La Flotte Byzantine á l'époque des Comnènes et des Anges (1081–1204)', *Byzantino-Slavica*, 21 (1960), pp. 48–53

Siberry, E., *Criticism of Crusading 1095–1274* (Oxford, 1985)

Sivan, E. (ed. and tr.) (al-Sulami, '*Kitab al-Jihad*'), 'Un traité Damasquin du début du XIIe siècle,' *Journal Asiatique*, 254 (1966), pp. 197–224

Southern, R.W., *Western Views of Islam in the Middle Ages* (Cambridge, MA, 1978)

Talmon-Heller, D., 'Muslim martyrdom and the quest for martyrdom in the Crusading period', *Al-Masaq*, 14 (2002), pp. 131–39

Tarsusi, 'Ali Ibn Murdi al- (tr. A. Boudot-Lamotte), *Contribution á l'Étude de l'Archerie Musulmane* (Damascus, 1968)

Taylor, W.R., 'A New Syriac Fragment Dealing with Incidents in the Second Crusade', *Annual of the American School of Oriental Research*, 11 (1929–30), pp. 120–30

Tritton, A.S., and H.A.R. Gibb, 'The First and Second Crusades from an Anonymous Syriac Chronicle (Part Two)', *Journal of the Royal Asiatic Society* (1933), pp. 273–305

Usamah Ibn Munqidh (tr. P.K. Hitti), *Memoires of an Arab-Syrian Gentleman* (New York, 1927; reprint Beirut 1964)

—— (tr. P.M. Cobb), *The Book of Contemplation: Islam and the Crusades* (London, 2008)

Von Kremer, A., *Topographie von Damas* (Vienna, 1854–55)

Wheeler, B., *Eleanor of Aquitaine: Lord and Lady* (London, 2003)

William of Tyre (tr. E. Babcock and A.C. Krey), *A History of Deeds Done beyond the Seas* (reprint New York, 1976)

Yared-Riachi, M., *La Politique extérieure de la principauté de Damas, 468–549H/1076–1154* (Damascus, 1997)

Yovitchich, C., 'La Citadelle de Bosra', in N. Faucherre et al. (eds.), *La Fortification au Temps des Croisades* (Rennes, 2004) pp. 205–17

Zanki, J.H.M.A. al-, *The Emirate of Damascus in the Early Crusading Period 488–549/1095–1153* (Ph. D. thesis, St. Andrews University, 1989)

INDEX